Documents in Contemporary History

General editor
Kevin Jefferys
Faculty of Arts and Education, University of Plymouth

War and reform

British politics during the Second World War

The Second World War marked a crucial watershed in the political history of modern Britain. This book seeks to explain, through the eyes of contemporaries, how the transition occurred from the Conservative 'enterprise society' of the 1930s to Labour's welfare state and mixed economy of the late 1940s. *War and reform* also addresses the question of how the political changes of this period affected British society as a whole and how much public opinion itself shaped change.

After introducing the main historical debates about British politics during the war, the editor draws upon a wide range of primary sources, including political diaries and letters, memoirs, newspaper articles, party manifestos and official government records. These are used to illuminate major developments of the 1939–45 period such as the downfall of Prime Minister Neville Chamberlain; the war leadership of Winston Churchill; the Beveridge Report and reconstruction; and the movement of popular opinion culminating in Labour's famous 1945 election victory.

War and reform provides a succinct guide to the latest academic research and a comprehensive selection of documentary extracts. The introductory section also discusses the methodological problems of primary source material and provides the ideal guide to the nature and uses of documentary evidence.

Documents in Contemporary History is a series designed for sixth-formers and undergraduates in higher education: it aims to provide both an overview of specialist research on topics in post-1939 British history and a wide-ranging selection of primary source material.

Forthcoming

Sean Greenwood *Britain and the European integration since the Second World War*

Steven Fielding *The Labour Party since 1951*

Stuart Ball *The Conservative Party, 1940–1992*

Chris Wrigley *British trade unions since 1945*

Harriet Jones *The politics of affluence, Britain 1951–64*

Rodney Lowe *The classic welfare state in Britain*

Documents in Contemporary History

War and reform

British politics during the Second World War

Edited by
Kevin Jefferys
Senior Lecturer in Contemporary History, University of Plymouth

Manchester University Press
Manchester and New York
Distributed exclusively in the USA and Canada by St. Martin's Press

Published by Manchester University Press
Oxford Road, Manchester M13 9NR, UK
and Room 400, 175 Fifth Avenue, New York, NY 10010, USA

Distributed exclusively in the USA and Canada
by St. Martin's Press, Inc., 175 Fifth Avenue, New York,
NY 10010, USAA

British Library Cataloguing-in-Publication Data
A catalogue record for this book is available from the British Library

Library of Congress Cataloging-in-Publication Data
War and reform : British politics during the Second World War / edited by Kevin Jefferys.
p. cm. — (Documents in contemporary history)
Includes bibliographical references and index.
ISBN 0–7190–3970–3. — ISBN 0–7190–3971–1 (pbk.)
1. Great Britain—Politics and government—1936–1945. 2. World War, 1939–1945—Great Britain. 3. World War, 1939–1945—Influence. I. Jefferys, Kevin. II. Series.
DA587.W28 1993
941.084—dc20 93–30885
CIP

ISBN 0–7190–3970–3 *hardback*
0–7190–3971–1 *paperback*

Typeset in Linotron Sabon
by Northern Phototypesetting Co. Ltd, Bolton
Printed in Great Britain
by Bell and Bain Ltd, Glasgow

Contents

List of illustrations

(All cartoons by David Low; reproduced with the permission of the *Evening Standard*).

Acknowledgements

For permission to reproduce copyright material, the publishers and editor would like to thank the following:

Sir Richard Butler (1.1, 4.3, 6.18); The British Library of Political and Economic Science (1.3, 1.15, 1.18, 1.20, 2.4, 2.11, 3.18, 4.11, 4.19, 6.10); Verily Anderson Paget (1.5); Mr Stanley Clement-Davies (1.5); David Higham Associates (1.6, 1.8, 2.16, 3.10, 4.12); the Rt. Hon. Lord Amery (1.9, 1.19, 2.1, 2.19, 6.14); Mr Nigel Nicolson (1.13, 2.14); the Rt. Hon. Paul Channon MP (1.10, 1.17, 2.2, 2.5, 2.17, 3.3, 3.6, 3.14); Hodder and Stoughton (1.22, 2.3, 2.15, 3.2, 4.2, 5.12, 6.1, 6.9); Captain J. Headlam and the Durham Record Office (2.13, 6.15); the Controller of Her Majesty's Stationery Office (3.4, 4.14, 5.3, 5.5); the Clerk of the Records, House of Lords Records Office (3.5); the Archive Trustees, Mass-Observation Archive, University of Sussex Reproduced by permission of Curtis Brown Ltd, London (3.7, 4.6, 5.2, 5.7, 5.11, 6.6); the Manuscripts Librarian, British Library (3.8, 3.19, 4.4, 4.9, 5.10, 6.16); the Master and Fellows of Trinity College, Cambridge (3.9, 4.15); *The Times* (4.1, 4.20); Tribune (4.7); © *The Economist* (4.16, 4.21, 5.9, 6.12); the estate of the late Sonia Brownell and Martin Secker & Warburg Ltd (5.4); *Peterborough Herald & Post* (5.8); Conservative Political Centre (6.7); the Labour Party (6.8); HarperCollins Publishers Limited (6.11, 6.17).

The cartoon by David Low on the cover, questioning whether hopes for post-war reform would be disappointed as they had after the 1914-18 war, first appeared in the *Evening Standard* on 8 March 1943. This and the Low cartoons in the text are all reproduced with the permission of the *Standard* and the Solo Agency, London.

Chronology of events

	Military	Political
1939		
September 1	German invasion of Poland.	
September 3	Britain declares war on Germany.	Prime Minister Neville Chamberlain reconstructs National government and appoints War Cabinet: Churchill as First Lord of the Admiralty.
September 22	Germany and Russia announce partition of Poland.	
September 27		Sir John Simon (Chancellor of the Exchequer) introduces first war budget.
1940		
April 9	Germany invades Norway and Denmark.	
May 2	British troops in Norway forced to withdraw.	
May 7–8		Norway debate in House of Commons – National government majority falls from over 200 to 81.
May 10	Hitler invades Belgium and Holland.	Chamberlain resigns and Churchill forms coalition. War Cabinet contains both Conservatives (Chamberlain, Lord Halifax) and Labour (Clement Attlee, Arthur Greenwood).

May 22		Emergency Powers Act passed, giving the government complete power over persons and property for the prosecution of war.
May 29	Evacuation of British forces from Dunkirk begins.	
June 17–22	Surrender of France.	
July–Sep.	Battle of Britain.	
October		Chamberlain resigns as leader of the Conservative party; replaced by Churchill.
December 22		Lord Halifax becomes British Ambassador to the United States; succeeded as Foreign Secretary by Anthony Eden.
1941		
January 21		Ernest Bevin, Minister of Labour, announces plans for the industrial conscription of all men and women.
April	German armies attack Yugoslavia and Greece; major withdrawal of Allied troops.	
May 8		Vote of confidence in House of Commons: only three MPs vote against the government.
June	Germans capture Crete; 15,000 British troops evacuated.	
22 June	Nazi attack on Soviet Union; Churchill pledges all possible assistance to the Russians.	
December	Japanese attack on Pearl Harbor brings the United States into the war.	

1942		
February 8		Sir Stafford Cripps, recently returned from Moscow, impresses the public with speech calling for Britain to match the commitment and sacrifice shown by the Russians.
February 15	British loss of Singapore announced.	
February 19		Government reshuffle: dismissal of both Tory and Labour ministers; Stafford Cripps enters War Cabinet.
March 25		Grantham by-election: first of five Conservative losses to Independent candidates.
June 21	British defeated at Tobruk in North Africa.	
July 1–2		Tobruk debate in parliament: vote of censure of Churchill defeated by 475 votes to 25, but with 30–40 abstentions.
November	Montgomery defeats Rommel at El Alamein.	
December 1		Publication of *Social Insurance and Allied Services* (the Beveridge Report).
1943		
February		Beveridge debate in House of Commons: Labour amendment calling for immediate implementation of Report defeated.
March 21		Churchill announces Four-Year Plan for reconstruction.
April 7		Eddisbury by-election: first of three Common Wealth successes.

July 16		Publication of white paper, *Educational Reconstruction*.
July	Downfall of Mussolini as Allies advance in Italy.	
November 11	Lord Woolton appointed Minister of Reconstruction.	
1944		
January 6		Conservatives lose Skipton by-election to Common Wealth.
February 17		West Derbyshire by-election: Tory loss to 'Independent Labour'. Publication of white paper, *A National Health Service*.
June 6	D–Day: major Allied landings in Normandy.	
June		Publication of white paper, *Employment Policy*.
August 3		Royal Assent given to Education Act: introduces free secondary schooling for all children over eleven.
September	Heavy losses at Arnhem hold up Allied advance against retreating German forces.	
October		Coalition deadlock over Town and Country Planning Bill.
1945		
February	Churchill, Roosevelt and Stalin discuss plans for peace at Yalta.	
May 7	Surrender of the German Supreme Command, following the suicide of Hitler.	
May 21		Labour conference agrees to leave the government.

May 23	Formal ending of the coalition; Churchill forms 'caretaker' administration: Chancellor Sir John Anderson; Foreign Secretary Anthony Eden.
July 5	Polling day for general election.
July 26	Announcement of election results: Labour 393 seats, Conservatives 213, Liberals 12; Attlee forms post–war Labour government.

Introduction

I

The Second World War transformed British politics. With the exception of two minority Labour governments, occupying a total of only three years, the Conservative party was continually in office – whether in its own right or as the dominant partner in a coalition – from the armistice of 1918 through to the outbreak of war against Nazi Germany in 1939. Tory electoral domination was based on an image of 'safety first': in the years after the First World War, the party of Stanley Baldwin and Neville Chamberlain offered a combination of fiscal prudence and cautious social progress. At the last general election before 'Hitler's war', held in 1935, the broad appeal of safety first was reaffirmed with a parliamentary majority of well over 200 seats for the National government. This Conservative-dominated coalition increasingly came under the sway of Chamberlain, a formidable Prime Minister from May 1937 onwards with a strong personal following among party loyalists. The Labour party, by contrast, remained very much the party of the urban, industrial working class, unable to attract sufficient middle-class backing to break the Tory stranglehold. At first sight, it was not obvious that the experience of a second war would break this pattern. After an upsurge of criticism about his handling of the war effort, Chamberlain resigned in favour of Winston Churchill, who invited the Labour opposition to join him in a government of national unity. Labour had suddenly gained a share in power, though it was not expected to last. Following Hitler's defeat five years later, the wartime coalition broke apart. Churchill, having established himself as the nation's inspirational leader, called upon the electorate to return him as head of a new Conservative administration.

He alone, the Prime Minister claimed, was capable of dealing with the domestic and international legacy left by six years of 'total war' against the Germans, Italians and Japanese. Among politicians and commentators, it was widely anticipated that Churchill would sweep back to power, just as Lloyd George had triumphed in 1918 as 'the man who won the war'. There was little reason to believe that the public would prefer the radical plans put forward by Labour and its enigmatic leader, Clement Attlee – 'Clem the Clam', as he was once called. The best Labour could hope for, it was believed, was to cut the size of the Conservative majority. But in the event the pundits were confounded. As the election results came through, it became apparent that the Labour party had won a landslide victory. Attlee's party secured nearly half the popular vote, winning 393 seats, compared with 213 for the Conservatives. On an average swing of twelve per cent, Labour benefited from one of the major upsets in modern electoral history, capturing scores of seats across the country that had never before returned a Labour member to the House of Commons. Hence it was not Churchill but the relatively unknown Attlee who became the nation's post-war premier. The war years thus marked a crucial watershed in the history of modern Britain: from the Conservative 'enterprise society' of the 1930s to the welfare state and mixed economy of the late 1940s; a new political order that was to prevail for a generation to come. This book seeks to explain, through the eyes of contemporaries, how such a transformation came about, and what its implications were for British society.

II

The primary sources used in this volume have been grouped together to follow the main phases, and highlight the main issues, of wartime politics. Chapter 1 addresses the theme of how a change of government came about in May 1940. The outbreak of war in 1939 dealt a severe blow to Neville Chamberlain, who had staked his reputation on preserving European peace through a policy of appeasement towards the Fascist dictators. When the so-called 'phoney war' came to an end in the spring of 1940, British military failure in Scandinavia provoked a domestic revolt. After the celebrated 'Norway debate' in the House of Commons (documents 1.11–16),[1] Chamberlain was forced to resign. It does not follow, as is often implied, that this resulted inevitably from the failure of appeasement. In practice the Prime Minister remained in a strong position (1.4) until influential members of his own party began to doubt his suitability as a war leader (1.8–9). Nor did the nation turn to Churchill as a saviour and 'man of destiny', the phrase he later used in his memoirs. There was great suspicion of Churchill within Conservative ranks because of his record of opposing the party leadership in the 1930s, and as diary extracts by his contemporaries show, Churchill ultimately succeeded because he proved most adept at ruthlessly exploiting Chamberlain's misfortune (1.9 and 1.20–21). The change of government that followed was to have a profound influence on the course of wartime politics: undermining the pre-war pattern of Tory domination and marking a vital breakthrough for Labour, foreshadowing the election landslide of 1945. Such an outcome, however, was impossible to predict on the day Churchill entered Downing Street, the same day that Hitler launched his blitzkrieg attack on the Low Countries. It was only much later, with the benefit of hindsight, that the importance of May 1940 as a turning point stands out.

The second chapter concerns itself with the period known as Britain's 'finest hour'. Churchill came to power at a time of desperate national crisis. In the weeks that followed, as British troops were forced to evacuate from the continent, his leadership proved to be critical in rallying the nation (2.4–5). After the defeat of the French army in June 1940, Britain was left to stand alone against the might of Nazi Germany. Invasion now looked to be inevitable, at least until the RAF succeeded in denying the Germans aerial supremacy over Britain during the long summer months. By the autumn, the Prime Minister was confident that survival was ensured. Although the civilian population faced untold new horrors in the Blitz, the prospect of invasion had receded – for good, as it turned out – and the government could begin considering ways of striking back. Ministers in the new coalition were naturally preoccupied with military strategy. But political developments behind the scenes were nevertheless more complex than popular mythology would suggest. As several diary records written at the time show, in the early weeks of his premiership Churchill was by no means a universally

[1] Hereafter documents are referred to by number only, e.g. (1.2).

acclaimed war leader (2.2 and 2.7–9). The legacy of Chamberlain's downfall was such that pre-existing tensions could not easily be forgotten, even at a moment of supreme crisis. In particular, most Conservative MPs – having faithfully backed Chamberlain and appeasement in the 1930s – only reluctantly came to terms with the new Prime Minister and the suddenly enhanced status of the Labour party (2.11–12). It was not until the end of a momentous year, after Chamberlain had died following a serious illness, that Churchill looked unassailable (2.19).

Chapter 3 illustrates how in the next phase of the war – during 1941–42 – military strategy became inextricably linked with war production. Britain's plight inevitably meant that domestic politics focused on how the nation's resources might be most effectively harnessed to achieve victory. 1941 was marked by a series of military reversals; as a result, friends and critics of the government alike became increasingly frustrated (3.2–5). Controversy over the 'production crisis', at first muted for fear of damaging national unity, gradually became more difficult to contain, especially after the entry of the Russians and Americans into the war raised expectations of ultimate victory. By early 1942 serious questions were being asked about Churchill's leadership. Military reverses in the Far East, and in particular the loss of Singapore to the Japanese, provided scope for renewed intrigue by the 'Chamberlainite' group still active on the 1922 Committee of Tory MPs (3.6 and 3.9). The Prime Minister's reaction to this build-up of pressure was to reorganise the War Cabinet, bringing in for example the emerging political figure of Stafford Cripps (3.7–8). The government reshuffle of February 1942 helped to shore up Churchill's authority, but left each major coalition partner convinced that the other was securing party advantage. Backbench discontent was the natural consequence of military defeat, and would persist for as long as the war continued to go badly. Hence a further challenge to the Prime Minister came after the Germans captured the North African fortress of Tobruk in June. Real anxiety amongst MPs was not fully reflected in the number of those voting against the government in the debate that followed (3.12–14), and Churchill remained worried that Stafford Cripps represented a genuine threat to his position (3.16–17). The situation was only resolved by a sudden improvement in Allied military fortunes. In November the British victory at El Alamein was followed by an Anglo–American offensive which decisively tipped the balance in North Africa, and in Eastern Europe the Russians showed signs of turning back Hitler's advance. The effect of this 'turn of the tide' on domestic politics was dramatic: overnight Churchill's critics were routed (3.18). His leadership, at last, was secure.

In the second half of the war, political attention at home centred on one main issue – reconstruction. The fourth chapter begins by noting that the government played down any real discussion of post-war prospects before the 'turn of the tide'. The Prime Minister was not only preoccupied with military matters, but believed that discussion of sensitive domestic issues might endanger the unity of the coalition (4.2–3). There was however increasing pressure for action, especially from Labour backbenchers (4.4). The whole course of the debate was suddenly placed on a new footing by the publication in December 1942 of the immensely popular Beveridge Report, (4.5) which called for an extensive new system of social security and a host of related reforms such as the introduction of a national health service and radically new employment policies. Churchill's fears about coalition discord appeared to be borne out when the major parties took very different views of the Report. The desire of Labour MPs to see reform implemented immediately led them to vote against the cautious position of the cabinet (and the Conservative party), thus openly dividing a coalition set up to demonstrate national unity (4.7–11). Enthusiasm for Beveridge did succeed in persuading the Prime Minister to take reconstruction more seriously, at least in public. Soon after this he announced his commitment to a Four-Year Plan, and followed it up with the appointment late in 1943 of a Minister of Reconstruction, charged with co-ordinating the various wide-ranging proposals for reform (4.12 and 4.17). But tangible results were slow in coming. By mid-1944 the government could boast an education bill (4.15) and a series of white papers, but after the D-Day landings in France brought the end of the war in sight, the problem of securing agreement between the two wings of the coalition became ever more acute (4.19–21).

As Allied victory became more certain, so speculation also increased about the likely pattern of post-war politics: would the coalition be extended beyond the end of the German war, and if so, for how long? The feeling that a complete return to conventional party politics was both desirable and inevitable increasingly took hold, and was first evident away from Westminster in the localities. This was ironic, for as chapter 5 indicates, in the emergency period of

1940–41, party competition had taken a back seat (5.2). Coalition leaders were bound throughout the war by the terms of an electoral truce, which outlawed Labour–Conservative by-election contests for the duration. This did not, however, prevent the emergence of new forces in British politics. With the war going badly, independent candidates began to topple government nominees in by-elections (5.6), and much publicity was accorded to the newly created Common Wealth party, whose unique brand of Christian socialism carried it to victory in Conservative-held seats during 1943–44 (5.7 and 5.10). The success of Common Wealth rapidly reinforced a countervailing trend: the tendency of many rank-and-file supporters to encourage a return to two-party politics. Labour activists in particular, sensing a swing to the left in the public mood, had always been unhappy with the electoral truce (5.3 and 5.5). As the war progressed, there were an increasing number of by-elections where the truce was breached in *de facto* party contests: perhaps the most notable example was the victory of an 'Independent Socialist' at West Derbyshire in February 1944 (5.8 and 5.11). West Derbyshire also focused the debate about what effects the war had produced on political allegiances. Was it only one of several signs of a profound shift to the left in public attitudes (5.13), or was it the case that Churchill's popularity as a war leader made the Conservative party unbeatable at any post-war election (5.9)?

This question was to be decisively answered at the 1945 election, which provides the theme of the final chapter. After the news of Germany's surrender came through in early May, attention at Westminster turned to the likely date of Britain's first general election for a decade. Most Conservatives favoured an early contest, hoping thereby to capitalise on Churchill's personal prestige. Labour leaders – also believing in the potency of the 'Churchill factor' – preferred a delay on tactical grounds, and so had some sympathy for the Prime Minister's offer to continue the coalition until the Japanese had been defeated. After the Labour conference voted against any such continuance, senior Tories were satisfied that they had won what amounted to the preliminary round of the election: placing the onus on Labour for forcing an early contest and leaving them open to the charge of preferring faction to unity at a time when international dangers remained acute (6.1). But in the campaign proper, the Conservatives were less fortunate. Churchill himself dismayed his followers – and many voters – with an opening broadside which argued that the introduction of socialism required 'some form of Gestapo' (6.3–6); a particularly tasteless remark at a time when the full atrocity of the concentration camps was becoming public knowledge. The tendency of Churchill's advisers to ignore major issues – such as whether public or private provision should take precedence after the war – created a belief that the Tory campaign lacked direction (6.9); an impression reinforced by the effort to whip up another 'scare story' in the final days before polling (6.10 and 6.12). Labour leaders were nevertheless taken aback when the scale of their victory became apparent in late July. As well as celebrating a famous triumph, many had to ask themselves whether it was 'all a dream' (6.16).

III

The distinct phases through which wartime politics passed can therefore be traced through a wide variety of documentary sources. Diaries or letters by leading politicians, public speeches, official government records, memoirs, newspaper articles, party manifestos, soundings of local opinion: all are represented in the chapters that follow. Each extract is briefly introduced, both as a means of providing background information and in order to highlight the problems raised by different types of evidence. Several of the autobiographical extracts used here, for example, provide wartime politicians with a retrospective opportunity to present their actions in the most favourable light. Diaries have the benefit of being written closer to the events described. But as many of the entries included here show – especially those by Labour's Hugh Dalton and the Conservative Henry Channon – diarists are equally prone to the grinding of particular axes. More balanced assessments can often be found in newspaper and journal articles, though most journalists, as will be seen, were as uncertain about shifts in popular attitudes as party politicians. Although much of the historical evidence used in this volume emanates from the 'high politics' world of Westminster, 'low politics' is not altogether ignored. Indeed the Second World War provided greater opportunities for the systematic recording of constituency opinion than in any pre-war generation. Concerned about public morale in the fight against Hitler, the government used various agencies – such as the Ministry of Information's Home

Intelligence Unit and the survey group Mass-Observation – to monitor attitudes to a wide range of issues, including politics.

But what have been the main debates among historians about wartime politics? Aside from the question of Chamberlain's downfall and replacement by Churchill, mentioned above, two broad historiographical issues perhaps stand out. The first, which is touched upon in chapters 3 and 4, concerns the significance of the war years for the longer-term development of British society. In a pioneering study first published in 1975, Paul Addison argued that the influence of Labour ministers in the coalition made the government the most radical since Asquith's Liberal administration in the Edwardian period. The war, he argued, placed on the agenda the major items of the post-war welfare state: social security for all, a national health service, full employment policies, improved educational opportunities and a new system of family allowances.[2] In looking beyond the official world of Whitehall, Addison claimed that both Conservative and Labour supporters committed themselves at the 1945 election to the principles of reconstruction endorsed by their leaders as members of the coalition. The war years thus produced a new political middle ground upon which the parties would henceforth compete for political power. In contrast to the negative hostility of the inter-war period, there was now emerging a common approach to welfare reform, a new and positive social policy 'consensus'. This new consensus fell, in a much-cited phrase, 'like a branch of ripe plums, into the lap of Mr Attlee'.[3] In subsequent writing, Paul Addison has qualified his use of the term 'consensus', preferring instead to speak of a 'post-war settlement'. But the idea of the war as a catalyst for change is reinforced with claims that the years after 1940 provided an administrative framework for reform by transforming the civil service, while also initiating a trend towards 'corporatism' in the British economy.[4]

The notion of a wartime consensus has certainly coloured an unfolding debate about the performance of the war economy. Keith

[2] Paul Addison, *The Road to 1945. British Politics and the Second World War*, London, 1975.

[3] Paul Addison, *The Road to 1945*, p. 14.

[4] Paul Addison, 'The road from 1945', in Peter Hennessy and Anthony Seldon (eds), *Ruling Performance. British Governments from Attlee to Thatcher*, Oxford, 1987.

Middlemas, for example, in a wide-ranging study of modern industrial politics, argues that corporatism originated in wartime circumstances: the product, he claims, of an alliance between government, employers and trade untions, forged initially to counter the Nazi threat but subsequently enshrined in the 1944 commitment to tackling unemployment.[5] This reading of the war years also underpins Corelli Barnett's controversial polemic, *The Audit of War*. Britain's post-war industrial decline, Barnett maintains, was rooted in the period when Churchill's coalition, instead of giving priority to much-needed economic regeneration, chose to focus instead on the creation of a social miracle, a 'New Jerusalem', evangelised by a motley collection of 'do-gooders'. According to Corelli Barnett, the opportunity was wasted to tackle the root causes of Britain's 'industrial disease', such as poor management and obstructive trade unions. Inevitably, as a result, the dreams of 1945 'turned to a dank reality of a segregated, subliterate, unskilled, unhealthy and institutionalised proletariat hanging on the nipple of state materialism'.[6] The 'Barnett thesis', however, has been fiercely challenged. His 'audit' has been attacked firstly for taking no account of the credit side of Britain's war economy. Although slow to mobilise, the British performance ultimately bore comparison with that of other major combatants; for instance a higher proportion of national income was devoted to the war than in either America or Russia.[7] Barnett has been criticised, secondly, for playing down the reasons for prioritising social reform, such as the mass destruction of housing by German bombing. And his assault on the 'wrong-turning' of a New Jerusalem has also been depicted as a red herring. Other European nations after 1945 managed to combine both increased welfare expenditure and industrial regeneration; in this sense the decision to create a welfare state cannot be arbitrarily blamed for Britain's poor economic performance.[8]

More recently some historians have questioned the whole idea of whether the war years really saw the creation of a new consensus.

[5] Keith Middlemas, *Power, Competition and the State*, Vol. I, *Britain in Search of Balance, 1940–1961*, London, 1986.

[6] Corelli Barnett, *The Audit of War: The Illusion and Reality of Britain as a Great Nation*, London, 1986, p. 304.

[7] Margaret Gowing, 'Britain's post-war industrial decline', *Contemporary Record*, 1, 2, 1987, p. 18.

[8] Jose Harris, 'Enterprise and the welfare state: a comparative perspective', in Terry Gourvish and Alan O'Day (eds), *Britain since 1945*, Basingstoke and London, 1991.

The period between 1939 and 1945, without doubt, witnessed considerable debate about the need for a new social order. Pressure for change emanated from a variety of sources. Away from Westminster, the lead was taken by writers and intellectuals, by much of the national press and by specialist pressure groups. But two recent studies have argued that such widespread pressure did not imply a new political consensus, either around the cabinet table or in the House of Commons and beyond amongst rank-and-file activists. There was certainly cross-party agreement about the need to defeat Hitler, but this was not extended to domestic issues, as became increasingly apparent after the turn of the tide in late 1942.[9] In this line of analysis, three particular points have been stressed about the coalition's reconstruction programme as it developed from early 1943 onwards. In the first place, the government deliberately limited its areas of domestic activity: on several topics where controversy threatened to erupt – for example over the future ownership of industry – ministers had to postpone the matter under discussion. Secondly, the proposals which the coalition did devise, mostly in the form of white papers, were not intended as binding commitments upon a future administration, and were sufficiently ambiguous to receive very differing interpretations on opposing benches in parliament. And finally, the reconstruction programme, in spite of the availability of parliamentary time, remained very much at the planning stage in 1943–44, with only an Education Act and family allowances reaching the statute book before the end of the war. Despite the appointment of a Minister of Reconstruction, the whole reform process increasingly came to a standstill as the imminence of military victory removed earlier imperatives for cross-party unity. Reconstruction, in short, never lived up to its initial promise.

The reason for this outcome, it has been argued, was clear-cut: it reflected at base, intractable differences between the major coalition partners. Some policy options were inevitably narrowed by wartime experience. But the differences between the parties remained profound. The Labour party was able to sharpen its commitment to economic planning and welfare reform as the political tide ran in its direction. By contrast, mainstream Conservative opinion had grave doubts about both the feasibility and desirability of creating a brave

[9] Kevin Jefferys, *The Churchill Coalition and Wartime Politics 1940–45*, Manchester, 1991; Stephen Brooke, *Labour's War. The Labour Party during the Second World War*, Oxford, 1992.

new world. This further helps to explain why there was no industrial restructuring of the sort favoured by Corelli Barnett. While squaring up to the external threat, neither side of industry could easily forget the bitter legacy of the inter-war years, and coalition industrial policy was inevitably based on a series of compromises between the supporters of capital and labour. Churchill's caretaker government, which would have shaped post-war policy had it been elected in 1945, as most commentators expected, was ambiguous about much of the coalition programme. For senior Tories, wartime proclamations were not seen as entailing binding commitments for the future. Rodney Lowe has argued that the Conservative party gradually adopted a new realism which included state intervention,[10] but this arguably applied only to a minority of backbenchers associated with education minister R. A. Butler, who later confessed that 1930s orthodoxy was not significantly eroded before 1945. For the majority of Conservative opinion – anticipating electoral victory under a revered war leader – there was no need to contemplate anything more than a superficial revision of domestic policy. The incentive to consider more far-reaching changes only came with the shock of a crushing electoral defeat in 1945. It follows that the creation of the mixed economy and the welfare state were not primarily the working out of agreed wartime reforms; they were ultimately dependent upon the particular aspirations of the post-war Labour government. The major features of the post-war settlement, the dispensation that was to preside for a generation to come, were forged after – and not before – the election of 1945.

IV

The events of July 1945 have also occasioned a second, largely separate, historiographical debate: what caused the Labour landslide? As several of the extracts in this volume indicate, there were clearly deep-rooted forces at work throughout the war years. Paul Addison pointed out in *The Road to 1945* how the Conservatives could be tarred with the brush of failing in office during the 1930s. Whatever the realities of social conditions before the war, Labour could make play with the idea that Toryism was associated with

[10] Rodney Lowe, 'The Second World War, consensus and the foundation of the welfare state', *Twentieth Century British History*, 1, 2, 1990, p. 162.

depression and mass unemployment; 'if you don't remember the 1930s', ran the Labour slogan, 'Ask your dad'. Neville Chamberlain, as we have seen, also received – whether rightly or wrongly – much of the blame for failing to prevent war, and the idea of the incompetent 'Men of Munich' had rapidly taken hold in the summer of 1940.[11] Again Labour stood to gain: by participating in the coalition, Labour could claim to be a patriotic party when the nation went to the polls in 1945. In addition to its pre-war record, a further explanation for the Conservative defeat is often said to lie in the nature of the conflict against Hitler, summed up in the notion of a 'people's war'. In an atmosphere of massive upheavals caused by bombing and industrial conscription, social distinctions began to break down and the demand for equality of sacrifice became intense. Although it would be easy to exaggerate the degree of social levelling that resulted, the trend towards egalitarianism could not be mistaken:

> In World War I the dominant ethos was one of traditional patriotism, with the emphasis upon the duty each man owed to his king and country. . . . In World War II the prevailing assumption was that the war was being fought for the benefit of the common people, and that it was the duty of the upper classes to throw in their lot with those lower down the social scale. Whenever there was a military setback, or a crisis in war production, resentment would break out against 'vested interests': people were alleged to be clinging to their privileges at the expense of the common good.[12]

But if these traditional explanations go far towards accounting for the swing to the left in the war years, they arguably do not tell the whole story. The fall of Chamberlain clearly marked a vital first blow to Conservative domination, though there are reasons for thinking that too much importance should not be attached to shifting attitudes in the early part of the war. Home Intelligence investigators, working for the government, found in 1941 that while there was already a strong feeling in favour of reducing class distinctions, there was also an 'absence of thought along conventional party lines'. And

[11] 'Men of Munich' refers to the Munich settlement of 1938, under which Chamberlain accepted Hitler's terms for a take-over of the German-speaking portion of Czechoslovakia.

[12] Addison, *Road to 1945*, p. 131. See also pp. 127–63 for the important chapter 'Two cheers for socialism, 1940–42'.

although Conservatives were suffering in by-election contests by 1942, this had to be set against the immense popularity of the Prime Minister. Why, after all, should the electorate, when eventually given a choice, prefer a Labour alternative whose leader seemed uninspiring? The answer to this question goes to the heart of coalition politics, and ties in with the theme of reconstruction already discussed. The swing to the left, it has recently been argued, can only be fully understood in two distinct phases. In the period 1940–42, the Conservatives as the majority party – and the party associated with the 'guilty men' – suffered in the eyes of the electorate for shortcomings in the nation's war effort. But the Tory malaise only deepened to a point where it became irreversible after 1943, when the Prime Minister shunned the opportunity of implementing far-reaching social change. The key moment, we might suggest, came with the government's response – or lack of it – to the Beveridge Report.

The desire of the British people to create a better world, though imprecise in many ways, could not be mistaken. But Churchill and his senior colleagues had little faith in the New Jerusalem. Above all, the coolness of Conservative ministers towards Beveridge proved to be profoundly damaging in the medium-term. The government's own sounding of popular feeling found that in nearly all parts of the country expectations were raised by the promise of the Beveridge reforms. This was soon overlaid, however, by anxiety that such reforms might never materialise, whether because of government attitudes, 'vested interests' or financial considerations. After the parliamentary debate of February 1943, when Labour backbenchers revolted against the procrastination of Tory ministers, public anxiety increased. Ministry of Information officials now found that majority opinion deplored what was seen as the shelving of the Report. Public feelings were said to vary from anger to despondency at this 'betrayal': 'Why', it was asked, 'get Beveridge to make a plan at all, if you are going to turn it down?' The government was now squarely blamed for creating a mood of cynicism about post-war intentions – a feeling that was to resurface during the remainder of the war, especially as Beveridge was turned into a white paper but not legislation. Signs of Conservative unpopularity gradually began to multiply. Opinion polls, though still in their infancy and not taken seriously by most politicians, gave Labour a lead of ten percentage points from 1943 onwards; and anti-Tory sentiment at by-elections such as Skipton and West Derbyshire was so pronounced as to be unmistakable. By its ambivalent attitude towards reconstruction, therefore, the Conservative party had thrown away its chance to shape and guide public expectations.[13]

The most recent studies of the 1945 election thus tend to highlight two conclusions. In the first place, it would be misleading to exaggerate the extent to which the war genuinely radicalised public opinion. There are dangers, as Tony Mason and Peter Thompson have pointed out, in suggesting that 'in 1945 people knew what they wanted – and what they wanted was contained between the covers of *Let Us Face the Future*', Labour's manifesto at the election.[14] Rather, as the Beveridge episode indicates, many voters were left cynical and disengaged from the political process. Though some were attracted by Labour's appeal as both a patriotic party and the party that could best deliver welfare reform, others were mainly protesting against the lack of direction shown by Tory leaders on the home front.[15] Any election inevitably contains a mixture of positive and negative reasons for voter preference, but insofar as 1945 represented a rejection of wartime Conservatism, then a second conclusion that is now more emphasised than in the past is Churchill's personal responsibility for the outcome. It was he above all who sought to pay no more than lip-service to the public concern about reconstruction, and it was he who scored own goals in the election campaign with his 'Gestapo speech' and pursuit of the Laski affair, thereby building up Attlee's reputation. If the Prime Minister had used the period after 1942 to forge a popular post-war policy, then wartime suspicions about the Conservative party might have been at least partially overcome. This is not to suggest that with different presentation the Tories would have won in 1945; but it could have been a closer run thing. As it was, the Prime Minister's handling of events helps to explain one of the major ironies of Britain's wartime experience: Winston Churchill, the great national hero who 'won the war', was the same party leader who 'lost the peace'.[16]

13 Jefferys, *Churchill Coalition*, pp. 138–63.

14 Tony Mason and Peter Thompson, ' "Reflections on a revolution"? The political mood in wartime Britain', in Nick Tiratsoo (ed.), *The Attlee Years*, London, 1991, p. 55.

15 Steven Fielding, 'What did "the people" want?: The meaning of the 1945 general election', *The Historical Journal*, 35, 3, 1992, pp. 623-39.

16 Jefferys, *Churchill Coalition*, p. 202.

1

The phoney war and the downfall of Neville Chamberlain

Hitler's invasion of Poland made certain Britain's entry into the Second World War. For several months, however, there were few major military engagements. As a result, Neville Chamberlain was easily able to contain critics of his reconstituted National government, especially as places had been found for the most noted 'anti-appeasers' of the 1930s, Winston Churchill and Anthony Eden. But as the extracts in this chapter show, by the spring of 1940 Chamberlain was increasingly criticised for lacking urgency, not only by the opposition Labour party, but also by traditionally loyal Conservative backbenchers. In May 1940, as British troops withdrew from Norway in the face of a German onslaught, feeling in the House of Commons reached such a pitch that the Prime Minister was forced to resign.

1.1 Chamberlain's declaration of war, September 1939

Britain's declaration of war on the morning of 3 September was immediately followed by an air-raid warning: an event later recalled with wry humour by R. A. (Rab) Butler, at the time a Conservative minister serving at the Foreign Office.

The Prime Minister's broadcast on the outbreak of war was pathetically moving, but scarcely a tocsin ringing to arms. However, none of us was obliged to comment on the spur of the moment; for he had hardly asked his colleagues how we liked it, when the air was rent by a terrible wailing which no wartime Londoner will ever forget. 'That is an air-raid warning', announced Chamberlain quite calmly. We all laughed, and someone said, 'It would be funny if it were'. He repeated several times, like a school-teacher dinning a lesson into a class of late developers, 'That is an air-raid warning'. Then Mrs. Chamberlain appeared in the doorway with a large basket containing books, thermos flasks, gas-masks and other aids to waiting, and everybody began to make their way to the War room through the basement of No. 10. I found myself alone in the Cabinet room. A few people were scurrying across Horse Guards to try to take shelter. I decided that I had better die in the Foreign Office and so walked slowly across Downing Street, which was by then deserted. Members of the Office had assembled in the basement; and we sat on the floor, there being no furniture. An officious warden told me that he did not anticipate the immediate use of gas. Neither, of course, did he anticipate that, without any intervening aerial bombardment, the sirens would soon be sounding the all-clear. That phase which was later to be called the phoney war (and by some humorists the 'bore war') had started with a phoney alarm.

Lord Butler, *The Art of the Possible*, London, 1971, p. 80.

1.2 The outbreak of war: unease in Conservative ranks

The day before Britain declared war there was anxiety in the House of Commons that Chamberlain appeared to be prevaricating in his response to Hitler's invasion of Poland. As these memories of one Conservative MP show, there was even a moment when it seemed that Tory 'anti-appeasers' might abandon their tradition of loyalty to the party leader.

The beginning of the second war was very different from that of the first. There were no cheering crowds this time. There was no enthusiasm. If any existed it would have been dimmed by the black-out which descended upon us even before the declaration of war. People acquired later the habit of coping with it. They grew accustomed to darkness and the electric torch lightened their way. . . .

The Prime Minister's statement in the House of Commons the following evening gave the impression to the whole House that even at this late hour Great Britain was going to repeat the surrender of

Munich. When Arthur Greenwood, acting leader of the Opposition, rose to reply, Amery shouted to him across the floor of the House, 'Speak for England', inferring that the Prime Minister had failed to do so.[1] Greenwood made a robust speech and was cheered by the Tories, who had listened to their own leader in embarrassed silence. . . .

At about 10.30 I went round to Winston's flat, which he had asked me to do. . . . He considered that he had been very ill-treated, as he had agreed the night before to join the War Cabinet but throughout the day he had not heard a word from the Prime Minister. He had wished to speak that night in the House but feeling himself already almost a member of the Government had refrained from doing so.

There were present at his flat Anthony [Eden], Bob Boothby, Brendan Bracken and Duncan Sandys.[2] We were all in a state of bewildered rage. Bob was convinced that Chamberlain had lost the Conservative Party forever and that it was in Winston's power to go to the House of Commons tomorrow and break him and take his place. He felt very strongly that in no circumstances now should Winston consent to serve under him. On the other hand, if Winston now backed Chamberlain he could save him. Was it better to split the country at such a moment or bolster up Chamberlain? That seemed at one time the decision Winston had to take.

To the accompaniment of a tremendous thunderstorm we talked and argued far into the night. At last we received information that when the House met at noon the following Sunday morning it would be announced that the country would be at war in the afternoon.

This altered the whole situation. Our heated discussion cooled down. Winston said that he would send in his letter (which he had just drafted) to the Prime Minister none the less, and so in the small hours we wandered home through the dark streets.

Duff Cooper, *Old Men Forget*, London, 1953, pp. 258–60.

[1] Arthur Greenwood, Deputy Leader of the Labour party, was standing in due to the absence through illness of Clement Attlee. Leo Amery, MP for Birmingham Sparkbrook, was a leading Conservative critic of Chamberlain's appeasement policy.

[2] Boothby, Bracken and Sandys were all Tory anti-appeasers closely associated with Churchill, who after years of exlusion from office now became First Lord of the Admiralty. Eden had hitherto been seen as the head of a separate group of backbench critics – the Edenites or 'glamour boys' as they were called by the Tory establishment.

1.3 The outbreak of war: Labour's reaction

The Labour opposition were invited by Chamberlain to join a new coalition government, but refused for reasons outlined here by one of the party's senior figures, Hugh Dalton, who recorded in his diary a conversation with the Tory minister Rab Butler.

. . . our attitude towards the Government is one of 'cold, critical, patriotic detachment'. Alternatively, we shall act as patriotic gadflies on ministers. We shall still be free to criticise if we think fit in the House, and the so-called 'political truce' whereby no contested elections take place for the time being, is subject to termination at any time at our discretion.

I speak to Butler in his room. . . . He asks why we decline to join the Government. I tell him that I will answer this question quite frankly. Having regard to our frequently expressed views of the P.M. and Simon,[3] we could not enter a Cabinet in which these two were Numbers 1 and 2. Moreover, we should require the influence of Sir Horace Wilson[4] to be eliminated. If we read that he had been appointed Governor of the Windward Islands and had already left England in order to take up this most respected position, we should be favourably impressed. (He asked whether we really attached as much importance to Wilson as this. I say, 'Yes, certainly, and I have so told a member of the War Cabinet, and one of my colleagues has so told another'.) Continuing, I point out that if, for instance, members of the Labour Party were given, say, one seat in the Inner Cabinet, plus the Postmaster-General and the Secretaryship of State for Latrines, we should not only be uninfluential within, but we should lose most of our power to exercise influence from without, since we should be continually referred to as 'Your Mr So-and-So, who is now a Secretary of State'. Further, we should lose much of our credit amongst our own people, who would be filled with suspicions at our official participation. He said that he agreed that these were weighty arguments.

[3] Sir John Simon, Chancellor of the Exchequer, and a stauch supporter of appeasement.

[4] Wilson was Permanent Head of the Civil Service.

B. Pimlott (ed.), *The Political Diary of Hugh Dalton 1918–40, 1945–60*, London, 1986: entry for 6 September 1939, p. 297.

1.4 The phoney war: containing the government's critics

Before Christmas 1939, ministers were not unduly worried by criticism from individual MPs, whether directed towards war strategy or domestic policy. The reasons behind such confidence are touched upon in this correspondence between one of Chamberlain's cabinet allies, the Lord Privy Seal, and Britain's ambassador to the United States.

There are, of course, a number of people who are asking whether it is worth while going on with a war that started to save Poland and has seen Poland's destruction in the course of three or four weeks. There are also people who are bewildered with the situation created by the Russian entry upon the West. There is a further class of those who are irritated by the smaller vexations of war, and who have not been braced up to them by any great demand for patriotic sacrifice. These classes of people must be constantly kept in mind. They do not, however, alter the fact that the morale of the country as a whole is good. Lloyd George[5] would not agree with me when I say this. He is out of touch with things; he hates the Government in general and Neville in particular, and feels bitterly that he has little or no chance of altering the course of things. The mistake that he made in the House on Tuesday was not that he came out for peace proposals, but that he implied that we were certain to be defeated, and that we must make peace from weakness and not from strength. I imagine the discontented in the country will rally round him, but I am sure that there is no big body of support that would influence the conduct of events in this direction. . . .

In the field of Home affairs, the Government's fortunes have been going rather better. It was inevitable that in a war in which there was little or no fighting, all the criticism would be concentrated upon the Home Front. The Opposition would not have been human if they had not seized every opportunity for discrediting the Government,

[5] David Lloyd George had been Liberal Prime Minister during the First World War. Out of office since the early 1920s, Lloyd George was a bitter opponent of Chamberlain, and was convinced by 1939 that Britain could not repeat its success of the Great War.

and the Press, deprived of their advertisements and betting news, found anti-Government stunts the best way to sell their papers. On the Government's side, there was little or no reply to these attacks. Everyone was working so hard that the defence went by default. Things have lately been going rather better. Some of the papers realise that they have overdone the criticism and, as a result of ten weeks of experience, the Government has been able to relax a number of the more irritating restrictions. One of the troubles is that the House of Commons has nothing to do except criticise the Government two or three days a week, and as the Government's legislative programme takes little or no time in the House, it means the fullest possible opportunity is given for nagging. I dare say that this criticism does not do much harm here, and I hope you will make it clear to our American friends that it is a part of the regular game and does not mean that the war is being incompentently carried on. As a matter of fact, an impartial observer would probably say that the war organisation has been too good rather than not good enough, and that the result has been that people have been annoyed by the working of a great machine whose full volume is only needed in a time of a hundred per cent war.

Samuel Hoare to Lord Lothian, 7 October and 11 November 1939, cited in Viscount Templewood, *Nine Troubled Years*, London, 1954, pp. 405–9.

1.5 The emergence of opposition to Chamberlain

In spite of ministerial confidence, back-bench concern about the government's handling of the war slowly began to build up in the early months of 1940.

At the beginning of the war the Opposition, as such, had ceased to exist. The feeling was that now that the war had broken out the duty of the Opposition was to assist as much as possible. This feeling was not shared, however, by all members of the Opposition or by some members of the Conservative Party, who still thought it was in the vital interest of the country to be as critical as possible, to keep the Government on its toes and ensure the maximum effort was given to the prosecution of the war.

Clement Davies, a Liberal backbencher, was convinced of this and for three or four months from the outbreak of war he was practically alone in the House on the stand he took against the Chamberlain Government. His view was that the Government had no conception of the magnitude of its task and completely under-rated the conditions. One example was an interview he had in the Reform Club with Leslie Burgin,[6] who told him that the war would not come, because Hitler was not in a position to fight a war as he lacked petrol and oil. He had only enough to last for six months – a perfect example of the incredible lack of imagination and understanding possessed by certain members of the Cabinet.

The first open attack Mr. Davies made was on Sir John Simon's first war Budget which he described as not a war Budget at all. He was budgeting as if the war would last only a few months, whereas Mr. Davies was certain it would last for years. . . .

Little by little a number of M.P.s from all sides of the House, principally Labour and Conservative, began to see things in the same light. Most prominent were Leo Amery, Bob Boothby, Duff Cooper and Attlee and Greenwood. This was around November, 1939, and February, 1940. They began meeting together in one of the House of Commons Committee rooms. They invited men in responsible positions in industry and commerce and in the Forces to come and give evidence before them. This formed the basis of a Vigilante Group and it became the nucleus of growing opposition to the Chamberlain Government.

'Memorandum on events leading to the downfall of Neville Chamberlain', written anonymously, no date: Clement Davies political papers, National Library of Wales, 1/2/8, pp. 1–2.

1.6 The war economy and the cabinet

One of the main priorities of government critics was to push for a single minister to oversee handling of the war economy; a proposal flatly rejected by Chamberlain in the House of Commons. The Prime Minister also feared Churchill's motives, according to the leader of the opposition Liberals, Sinclair,

[6] Minister of Supply in the reconstituted National government of September 1939.

talking here with the editor of the *Manchester Guardian*, W.P. Crozier.

11.45 a.m. Sir Achibald Sinclair

He said that the appointment of an Economic Minister to the War Cabinet must come and in his opinion it was badly needed. I mentioned Sir Andrew Duncan's name[7] and he said he thought he was a possibility as he was well spoken of in every quarter. There was, however, a 'solid group' in opposition to the idea; it consisted of Chamberlain, Simon and Horace Wilson. Simon was determined to hold on to power; Chamberlain was thorougly self-satisfied and Wilson was now an immense power behind the throne in all directions. Wilson was specially active with regard to appointments and promotions and he had reason to believe that he was keeping out people who had been opposed to Chamberlain's Munich policy. He thought that we might hear more on this point before long and he would keep me informed.

When we began to talk about the question of a smaller Cabinet, he said that he would tell me the inner history of the formation of the present Cabinet at the beginning of September. Actually Chamberlain was not then opposed to the idea of a small Cabinet; until 2 p.m. on the Sunday, the day when war was declared, the Inner Cabinet was to consist of six people only, and these were to be Chamberlain, John Simon, Hankey, Chatfield, Halifax,[8] and Winston Churchill without a department; Samuel Hoare was not at that stage included. Before 2 p.m. the Chief Tory Whip (Margesson)[9] had told the Labour leaders that this was to be the Government and that it would be announced in this form about 5 p.m. When the announcement was actually made at five it was found that the War Cabinet consisted of nine members including all of the service Ministers. The Labour men to whom Margesson had spoken reproached him for milseading them and said it was rather awkward for them. Margesson replied that the reason for the change was that Churchill, if he were in the War Cabinet without a department to occupy him, would be 'too dangerous'. . . .

[7] Duncan was a leading industrialist, at the time Chairman of the Iron and Steel Trades Confederation.

[8] In the War Cabinet, Lord Hankey became Minister without Portfolio, Lord Chatfield Minister for Defence and Lord Halifax the Foreign Secretary.

[9] David Margesson, Conservative MP for Rugby since 1924.

A. J. P. Taylor (ed.), *W. P. Crozier. Off the Record. Political Interviews 1933–1943*, London, 1973: interview dated 16 February 1940, pp. 137–8.

1.7 'The Four Horsemen of the Apocalypse'

Anxiety about the government's handling of the war economy became widespread, as reflected in this cartoon by David Low. The fourth horseman depicted here was Colonel Blimp, a character created by Low to represent reactionary forces in 1930s Britain.

David Low, The Four Horsemen of the Apocalypse, *Evening Standard*, 25 April 1940.

1.8 'The House of Commons was no good'

As a member of the Chamberlain cabinet, Churchill was unable to voice any reservations he might have about the war effort. His close ally, Brendan Bracken, was bound by no such constraints, and his diatribe here to the editor of the *Manchester Guardian* highlights the deep divisions that still existed between the pro- and anti-appeasement wings of the Conservative party.

5.00 p.m. Brendan Bracken at the Admiralty

Things were rotten, and they were getting worse. We were not winning this war, we were on the way to [losing] it. The House of Commons was no good, the Tory party were tame yes-men of Chamberlain. One hundred and seventy had their election expenses paid by the Tory Central Office and 100 hoped for jobs; what independence or criticism, then, could be expected? The M[anchester] G[uardian] stuff about Margesson and the 'gag' was first-rate and it was all true. It was impossible to get rid of the notorious duds in the Ministry; Chamberlain and those round him could not be budged. The state of shipping was worse than supposed. Air production was not good. I said, why? and he answered – personal differences between the professionals at the top and Kingsley Wood[10] no good at putting his foot down and deciding. There were differences of opinion about new types and KW could not settle them. We had been promised that before long our single output should be equal to that of Germany and now we were told that the output of Britain and France and planes brought from USA were equal to that of Germany! If any Tory rank and file dared to raise their voice against the Government, they ran away the next day, and it was much worse now the war was on: e.g. on Palestine in June last year the Government had a majority of 80 and now it rose to 200 or thereabouts. Margesson was largely to blame; he had declared, in respect of some man who had criticised the Government, that he would give nothing to any critic of the Government if he could help it. I asked him if he had read the *Telegraph* leader today saying private members must not express opinions that would endanger the Government and he said 'I hope you'll give them hell!'

Taylor (ed.), *Off the Record*: W. P. Crozier interview dated 29 March 1940, p. 156.

[10] Secretary of State for Air and a close ally of Chamberlain in the 1930s.

1.9 The formation of the 'Watching Committee'

By the spring of 1940 the feeling that the government lacked urgency was spreading to the ranks of those within the Conservative party who had hitherto been loyal Chamberlainites; the Watching Committee was set up as a means of influencing ministers behind the scenes. Insertions in the text here appear in the published Amery diary.

To the House where I presently addressed a not very large meeting of Clement Davies' ginger group on our general progress with the war up to date, emphasising the fact that the Germans had probably widened the gap between ourselves and them on land and in the air. . . . Then to Arlington Street where Salisbury had convened an initial meeting of the proposed Watching Group of Government supporters from both Houses. The Lords were well-represented [they included Cecil, Horne, Hailsham, Lloyd, Swinton, Londonderry and Trenchard] and the Commons divided between good boys [i.e. pro-Chamberlain] like [Patrick] Spens, [Sir Joseph] Nall, Geoffrey Ellis and bad ones like Macmillan, Law, myself, Emrys Evans [and Wolmer, Harold Nicolson and Spears] the last named of whom was made Secretary.[11] We got almost at once on to the subject of a proper War Cabinet, Philip Swinton[12] and myself sustaining the case for it from our own experience. Practically all the Peers for it, but one or two of the Commoners like Spens and Nall, doubtful. Other subjects under discussion were strategy, economics and the home front.

J. Barnes and D. Nicholson (eds), *The Empire at Bay: the Leo Amery Diaries 1929–1945*, London, 1988: entry for 4 April 1940, p. 585.

1.10 Churchill, Chamberlain and the Norway expedition

According to this diary record by a staunch back-bench supporter of Chamberlain, it was as Britain's first serious military

[11] All those listed here were Conservative/National peers or MPs; by bad boys Amery meant those viewed with suspicion because of their opposition to appeasement.

[12] Formerly Philip Cunliffe-Lister, a senior Tory minister in the 1930s.

encounter of the war began to go wrong that the seeds of a political crisis were sown.

The House was crowded and pleasant and I was surrounded by people all day, which always stimulates me. Dunglass[13] pumped me: did I think that Winston should be deflated? . . . Ought he to leave the Admiralty? Evidently these thoughts are in Neville's head. Of course he ought to go, but who could we replace him with? Today I heard that chagrined by his failure at the Admiralty, he has now thrown off his mask, and is plotting against Neville, whom up to now he has served loyally; he wants to run the show himself: all this was inevitable, and I am only surprised it did not come before. Winston, it seems, has had secret conversations and meetings with Archie Sinclair, A. V. Alexander[14] and Mr Attlee and they are drawing up an alternative Government, with the idea of succeeding at the first favourable moment. . . .

It was decided to send Kingsley [Wood] to No. 10 at ten o'clock to warn the PM and consult him. He did, and the PM was shaken and indignant. So now we are in for a first-class political struggle between the Chamberlain men and the 'glamour' group: we may weather the storm, but there is trouble ahead all of which of course can only cause glee in Germany.

While these intrigues are going on our position in Norway is terrible, desperate, far worse than the public realises. . . .

R. Rhodes James (ed.), *Chips. The Diaries of Sir Henry Channon*, London, 1967: entries for 25–26 April 1940, pp. 242–3.

1.11 Evacuation of British troops in Norway

Unlike the public, MPs were rapidly becoming aware that British forces faced humiliation at the hands of the Germans in Scandinavia. The effect this news had on the various disaffected groups is recorded here by a promiment back-bench member of the Watching Committee.

[13] Lord Dunglass, later Alec Douglas-Home, the Prime Minister's Parliamentary Private Secretary.

[14] Albert Alexander, Labour MP for Hillsborough.

Tuesday, 30th April. Watching Committee met at six o'clock at Arlington Street. Astor Group dinner at the House of Commons. . . . The Chief Whip (David Margesson) appeared at dinner unexpectedly and as far as I could make out tried to forestall any inconvenient discussion by talking himself most of the time. The Government was obviously very unhappy about the Norwegian expedition, and it looked as if they were trying to throw the responsibility onto Winston. The evacuation of Norway was certain.

Wednesday, 1st May. Dinner, Carlton Hotel, Amery Group. It was clear that all question of throwing the blame for Norway on Winston had been abandoned. The Government were now sheltering behind him. Brendan Bracken again came in after dinner and we told him that we thought a new Government was absolutely essential. Either an interim Government under Halifax, or else a new Government under Winston.

Thursday, 2nd May. Evacuation of the force south of Trondheim announced by the P.M. and arrangements made for a debate on Tuesday and Wednesday of the following week. I went up to the House of Lords and saw Lord Salisbury and a small meeting of peers belonging to the Watching Committee assembled in the Moses Room. It was clear that a serious political crisis was developing.

Diary of Paul Emrys Evans MP: Emrys Evans papers, British Library Add. Mss. Vol. 58246, ff. 123–4.

1.12 First day of the Norway debate: Chamberlain's defence

As parliament met to discuss the British expedition in Norway, the Prime Minister remained confident of containing his critics. His speech opening the debate sought to lower the temperature by playing down the seriousness of any military reverses.

First of all, I want to ask hon. Members not to form any hasty opinions on the result of the Norwegian campaign so far as it has gone. . . . It is too early to say on which side the balance will finally incline. I may remind the House that the campaign is not yet finished. . . .

That brings me to the second point that I want to make. Germany, with her vast and well equipped armies, is so placed that she can at any moment attack any one or a number of points. We want to be ready to meet the attack wherever it may come. . . . A minister who shows any sign of confidence is always called complacent. If he fails to do so, he is labelled defeatist. For my part I try to steer a middle course – [Interruption – Hon. Members: 'Hitler missed the bus'][15] neither raising undue expectations, nor making the people's flesh creep by painting pictures of unmitigated gloom.

Once again I want to urge hon. Members that in these strenuous days we should do better to occupy ourselves with increasing our war effort than disputing about the form of Government. . . . The co-operation of Members of all parties, if not the co-operation of all Members of all parties, is a work which everyone recognises to be the prime need today. . . . Let us then before these trials come upon us put all our strength into the work of preparing for them, and we shall thus steadily increase our strength until we are ourselves are able to deliver our blows where and when we will.

Hansard, *Parliamentary Debates*, fifth series, vol. 360, 7 May 1940, c[olumns] 1081–6.

1.13 First day of the Norway debate: Chamberlain under attack

The Prime Minister's confidence appears to have been misplaced when he is followed in the debate by a series of highly critical speakers, as recorded here in the diary of one unsympathetic MP.

The House is crowded, and when Chamberlain comes, he is greeted with shouts of 'Missed the bus!' He makes a very feeble speech and is only applauded by the Yes-men. He makes some reference to the complacency of the country, at which the whole House cheers vociferously and ironically, inducing him to make a little, rather feminine, gesture of irritation. Attlee makes a feeble speech and Archie Sinclair a good one. When Archie sits down, many people stand up and the Speaker calls on Page Croft.[16] There is a loud moan from the Labour Party at this, and they practically rise in a body and leave the

[15] An ironic reference by Labour MPs to a speech in which Chamberlain said that by not attacking earlier, the Germans had 'missed the bus'.

[16] Sir Henry Page Croft, Conservative MP for Bournemouth.

House. He is followed by Wedgwood[17] who makes a speech which contains everything that he ought not to have said. He gives the impression of being a little off his head. At one moment he suggests that the British Navy have gone to Alexandria since they are frightened of being bombed.

A few minutes afterwards Roger Keyes[18] comes in, dressed in full uniform with six rows of medals. I scribble him a note telling him what Wedgwood has just said, and he immediately rises and goes to the Speaker's chair. When Wedgwood sits down, Keyes gets up and begins his speech by referring to Wedgwood's remark and calling it a damned insult. The Speaker does not call him to order for his unparliamentary language, and the whole House roars with laughter. . . . Keyes then returns to his manuscript and makes an absolutely devastating attack upon the naval conduct of the Narvik episode and the Naval General Staff. The House listens in breathless silence when he tells us how the Naval General Staff had assured him that a naval action at Trondheim was easy but unnecessary owing to the success of the military. There is a gasp of astonishment. It is by far the most dramatic speech I have ever heard, and when Keyes sits down there is thunderous applause.

Thereafter the weakness of the Margesson system is displayed by the fact that none of the Yes-men are of any value whatsoever, whereas all the more able Conservatives have been driven into the ranks of the rebels. A further terrific attack is delivered by Amery, who ends up by quoting Cromwell, 'In the name of God, go!'

N. Nicolson (ed.), *Harold Nicolson. Diaries and Letters 1939–1945*, London, 1967: entry for 7 May 1940, pp. 76–7.

1.14 First day of the Norway debate: 'the dagger in the heart'

Although the above extract focuses on the speech by Roger Keyes, it was widely believed that the most damaging attack on the Prime Minister came from Leo Amery, one of his close associates in earlier days as a fellow Birmingham MP. His famous speech was later described by Chamberlain's own

[17] Josiah Wedgwood, Labour MP for Newcastle under Lyme.
[18] Admiral of the Fleet Sir Roger Keyes, Tory MP for Portsmouth North.

parliamentary secretary as the real 'dagger in the heart'.[19]

This afternoon, as a few days ago, the Prime Minister gave us a reasoned, argumentative case for our failure. It is always possible to do that after every failure. Making a case and winning a war are not the same thing. Wars are won, not by explanations after the event but by foresight, by clear decision and by swift action. I confess that I did not feel there was one sentence in the Prime Minister's speech this afternoon which suggested that the Government either foresaw what Germany meant to do . . . or acted swiftly or consistently throughout the whole of this lamentable affair.

We cannot go on as we are. There must be a change. First and foremost, it must be a change in the system and structure of our governmental machine. This is war, not peace. . . . What we must have, and have soon, is a supreme war directorate of a handful of men free from administrative routine, free to frame policy among themselves, and with the task of supervising, inspiring and impelling a group of departments clearly allocated to each one of them. That is the only way. We learned that in the last war. . . .

What is no less important today is that the Government shall be able to draw upon the whole abilities of the nation. It must represent all the elements of real political power in this country, whether in this House or not. . . . The time has come, in other words, for a real National Government. . . .

Just as our peace-time system is unsuitable for war conditions, so does it tend to breed peace-time statesmen who are not too well fitted for the conduct of war. Facility in debate, ability to state a case, compromise and procrastination are the natural qualities of a political leader in time of peace. They are fatal qualities in war. Vision, daring, swiftness and consistency are the very essence of victory. . . . Somehow or other we must get into the Government men who can match our enemies in fighting spirit, in daring, in resolution and in thirst for victory. . . .

It may not be easy to find these men. They can be found only by trial and by ruthlessly discarding all who fail and have their failings discovered. We are fighting today for our life, for our liberty, for our all; we cannot go on being led as we are. I will quote some words from Oliver Cromwell. I do so with great reluctance, because I am

[19] Lord Home, *The Way the Wind Blows*, London, 1976, p. 74.

speaking of those who are old friends and associates of mine, but they are words which, I think, are applicable to the present situation. This is what Cromwelll said to the Long Parliament when he thought it was no longer fit to conduct the affairs of the nation: 'You have sat too long here for any good you have been doing. Depart, I say, and let us have done with you. In the name of God, go'.

Hansard, *Parliamentary Debates*, fifth series, vol. 360, 7 May 1940, cc. 1141–50.

1.15 Second day of the Norway debate: the Labour view

Emboldened by Amery's speech, the Labour opposition decided to turn the debate into a vote of confidence in Chamberlain, having hitherto held back for fear of rallying all Tory MPs behind their party leader. This decision clearly rattled the Prime Minister, who made an unfortunate intervention on the second day of the debate that further undermined his cause.

At 10.30 this morning Parliamentary Executive meets and we discuss whether or not to take a vote tonight on the adjournment. A better discussion than usual. . . . My view is that there are strong arguments on both sides, but that a vote at this stage is likely to consolidate the Government majority and that Chamberlain and Margesson would like us to have one. At the Party Meeting later in the morning the Executive recommendation to have a vote is accepted, though with some doubts and dissentients. Later events prove that this was quite the right decision, and that my judgement was wrong.

Today's debate is very dramatic. Morrison[20] opens very well, though somewhere in the middle of his speech he lost grip for a while, but he has lots of detail and is very definite. He again names Chamberlain, Simon and Hoare as men who must go. He ends up by saying that we shall vote. Thereupon, when he sits down, up jumps the Old Man, showing his teeth like a rat in a corner, and says 'I accept the challenge. . . . No Government can continue unless it has the support of Parliament and the public. I ask my friends – and I still have some friends in this House – to support the Government tonight in the Lobby.' He then sat down and Hoare began to speak about the

[20] Herbert Morrison, a senior figure on Labour's front-bench.

Air. The Old Man's intervention was gawky in its appeal to his 'friends', as Lloyd George and others rubbed in later on.

Pimlott (ed.), *Political Diary of Hugh Dalton*: entry for 8 May 1940, pp. 340–1.

1.16 Second day of the Norway debate: the Tory rebel view

Conservative MPs now had to decide whether to break with their tradition of always supporting the leadership at crucial moments. As this extract shows, the feeling on the Watching Committee – and amongst those serving in the armed forces – was that things had gone too far for Chamberlain to buy off his opponents with promised concessions.

The Watching Committee met at eleven o'clock at Arlington Street. Lord Salisbury went over his speech which was strongly supported by the committee. At lunchtime it was announced that the Labour Party proposed to challenge a division. Lord Salisbury had expressed the view that in the event of a division the Conservative critics should abstain. When the House met it was clear, however, that a large number of Tory Members, particularly Service Members, had made up their minds to go into the lobby against the Government. . . .

Alec Dunglass (the P.M.'s Parliamentary Private Secretary) asked me whether my friends would vote for the Government, on the understanding that we should see the P.M. the following morning and place any demands which we wished to make before him. He implied that the P.M. was prepared to carry out a drastic reconstruction of the Government. I told him that it was too late. I said that the Government could have been reconstructed at the beginning of the War or even as late as Christmas; we were thorougly dissatisfied with Ministers such as Simon and Hoare, and with Sir Horace Wilson and his intolerable interference and evil influence on policy. I also explained that the attitude of the Whips Office had been disastrous and that we did not think the P.M. had the right temperament for a Head of Government in wartime. I nevertheless promised to put his proposals before my friends, and a meeting was summoned for 9 o'clock that night.

In the meantime, Duff Cooper made a most powerful speech

asking for the dismissal of the Government, and announcing he would vote against it. At 9 o'clock the Conservative critics met and were joined by Clement Davies and his friends. It was decided to vote against the Government, and I informed Alec Dunglass of our decision. Dick Law[21] and I saw Brendan Bracken in Winston's room at the House, and he told us that it was unlikely that Winston would be prepared to serve under Halifax. Winston wound up for the Government in a brilliant speech, the whole of which was devoted to Norway with the exception of the last three minutes. (L.G. had urged him not to become an 'air raid shelter' for the Government, and he didn't).

Emrys Evans diary, 8 May 1940: British Library Add. Mss Vol. 58246, ff. 125–6.

1.17 Second day of the Norway debate: the Tory loyalist view

The climax of the debate came with an ironic speech from Churchill, defending the government as First Lord of the Admiralty, even though he seemed a likely beneficiary of Chamberlain's discomfort. The dramatic scenes as Tory MPs went into different lobbies for the vote were vividly described by one of the Prime Minister's distressed supporters.

The cataclysmic day has drawn to a welcome close and I am worn out, revolted by the ingratitude of my fellow-men, nauseated by the House of Commons, which I really think ought, though I love it, to be abolished. When I got there the atmosphere of the House was definitely excited and it intensifed as the long hours passed. Herbert Morrison opened the debate with vituperation, and announced that the Opposition would challenge the Government into a division. The PM, angry and worn out, intervened to say that the Government accepted the challenge, and he called upon his friends to rally round and support him. Possibly he was tactless, but I do not quite see what other course he could have followed. We knew then that it was to be war. . . . The temperature rose, hearts hardened, tempers sharpened, and I came to the conclusion that there is nothing so revolting as the

[21] Richard Law, Conservative MP for Hull South-West.

House of Commons on an ugly night. Little Neville seemed heart-broken and shrivelled. . . .

The real issue of the Debate – Norway – had long since been forgotten: speakers attacked us on any possible ground, and still the doubt was in everybody's mind, would Winston be loyal? He finally rose, and one saw at once that he was in bellicose mood, enjoying himself, relishing the ironical position in which he found himself: i.e. that of defending his enemies, and a cause in which he did not believe. He made a slashing, vigorous speech, a magnificent piece of oratory. . . . Winston told the story of the Norwegian campaign, justified it, and trounced the Opposition, demolishing Roger Keyes etc. How much of the fire was real, how much ersatz, we shall never know, but he dazzled everyone with his virtuosity. . . .

At last the Speaker called a division, which Winston nearly talked out. I went into the Aye Lobby, which seemed thin for a three line Whip, and we watched the insurgents file out of the Opposition Lobby. . . . 'Quislings',[22] we shouted at them, 'Rats'. 'Yes-men', they replied. . . . 'We are all right' I heard someone say, and so it seemed as David Margesson came in and went to the right, the winning side of the table, followed by the other tellers. '281 to 200' he read, and the Speaker reported the figures. There were shouts of 'Resign-Resign' . . . and that old ape Josh Wedgwood began to wave his arms about and sing 'Rule Brittania'. Harold Macmillan,[23] next to him joined in, but they were howled down. Neville appeared bowled over by the ominous figures, and was the first to rise. He looked grave and thoughtful and sad: as he walked calmly to the door, his supporters rose and cheered him lustily and he disappeared. No crowds tonight to cheer him, as there were before and after Munich – only a solitary little man, who had done his best for England.

What can Neville do now? He can reconstruct his Government; he can resign: but there is no dobut that the Government is seriously jarred and all confidence in it is gone.

Rhodes James (ed.), *Channon Diary*: entry for 8 May 1940, pp. 245–7.

[22] A term of abuse implying that MPs voting with the opposition were – like the Norwegian Fascist Quisling – doing Hitler's dirty work for him.

[23] Conservative MP for Stockton and a noted anti-appeaser.

1.18 Aftermath of the debate: could Chamberlain survive?

In spite of the loss of confidence among his own supporters manifest in the House, Chamberlain spent the following day seeking ways of continuing as Prime Minister.

House in a buzz. Boothby says most of the 43 of last night met today and decided not to join or support any government which did not contain members of the Labour and Liberal Parties; also to serve under any Premier who could create such a government. He asked would it help to publish this? I said yes, certainly; no member of our Party would serve under Chamberlain, nor, I thought, with Simon or Hoare. With these three out, on the other hand, we should be prepared to discuss, and to accept our full share of responsibility on proper terms. Later, I saw him surrounded by the press. The Old Man was telephoning personally from 8 a.m. onwards, trying to conciliate opponents of yesterday. He seems determined himself to stick on – like a dirty old piece of chewing gum on the leg of a chair, as someone said – but is offering to get rid of Simon, Hoare, and, if need be, Kingsley Wood, if this would propriate critics. It will not. Last night's division, and especially the large number of young men in uniform in our Lobby, has shattered them. Wise[24] said to me today, 'I have come straight back from from Namsos to vote against the Government. I voted on behalf of my men. We were bombed by German aeroplanes and had nothing with which to reply, not even a machine gun. When I went back last night to the Mess, everyone, from the Major General downwards, said Well done!'

Pimlott (ed.), *Political Diary of Hugh Dalton*: entry for 9 May 1940, p. 343.

1.19 The Prime Minister on the way out

After exploring all the options for remaining in office, such as inviting Labour once more to join a coalition, the message gradually sunk in that Chamberlain's opponents would be satisfied with nothing less than his own departure.

[24] Alfred Wise, Tory MP for Smethwick.

Early meeting of Salisbury's Watching Committee at which general feeling was, including those who had voted with the Government, that Neville should now resign and either Halifax or Winston form a real War Cabinet on National lines though not a Whips' War Cabinet but one selected by the new Prime Minister on merit, and Salisbury was deputed to go and convey this to Halifax. . . .

Soon after I got back Gibson[25] came round in a great state having just heard at the Cabinet Offices that Horace Wilson was proposing, as a solution of the crisis, that Neville should offer me some office and Gibson was terrified lest I should accept. This is truly typical of the Horace Wilson methods and of the kind of opinion Neville's advisers have held as to the motives which inspired criticism and opposition. Heard a good bit from Clem Davies who has been very active in constant touch with the Labour leaders, of the meetings between them and Neville that afternoon. Neville, who was accompanied by Winston and Halifax, received Attlee and Greenwood and began by saying that he thought the time had come to renew his offer of last autumn to invite the Opposition to join his government. This completely flabbergasted Attlee but Greenwood took up the running and explained that the Prime Minister was entirely mistaken and that there was not the slightest prospect of the Opposition joining a government under him; they not only disliked him but regarded him as something evil. . . . The interview thus closed, Neville apparently for the first time realising that he might have to go.

Barnes and Nicholson (eds), *Amery Diaries*: entry for 9 May 1940, pp. 611–13.

1.20 Chamberlain's resignation: the role of the Labour party

News of the German attack on the Low Countries gave Chamberlain one last hope of clinging to power. But when Labour leaders – en route to the party conference meeting in Bournemouth – made it clear that this new emergency only heightened the need for change, the Prime Minister had no choice but to tender his resignation.

[25] One of Amery's close associates.

This morning Hitler violated Holland, Belgium and Luxemburg. Should Parliament meet?. . . . I hold strongly that it should not, for this would give the cheer-leaders and crisis-exploiters a chance to rehabilitate the Old Man. All N[ational] E[executive][26] members due to leave for Bournemouth by 11.34 a.m. train. I go round to House of Commons at 10 and see Attlee who arrives about 10.30. Greenwood also comes in later. We all agree that we should not ask for Parliament and should go to Bournemouth. Attlee and Greenwood had seen the Old Man last night, when he had once more begged them to enter a Government under his premiership. They had told him bluntly that this was impossible and that the mood of the country required a new premiership. He then asked would we serve under a new Premier. They said they could give no answer to this before consulting colleagues. He asked for an early and definite answer to this last question and also to the first which he had put, namely, would we serve under him. He had also asked whether, pending an answer to these two questions, we would not send a message saying that the Labour Party supported the Government at this grave crisis of the war. This old man is incorrigibly limpet and always trying new tricks to keep himself firm upon the rock. . . .

Arrived at Bournemouth, the N.E. met and without too long discussion, even though many were more talkative than usual, being in a state of excitement, decided unanimously that we were prepared 'to take our share of responsibility in a new Government which, under a new Prime Minister, would command the confidence of the nation'. We also decided that Attlee and Greenwood should go forthwith to London to carry on any negotiations necessary to implement this decision, and that it was a decision and not merely a recommendation to the Conference on the following Monday, it now being Friday. This, we said, is a time when we must act swiftly and show leadership. As Attlee and Greenwood were about to leave, the P.M.'s Secretary rang through to enquire whether we yet could answer his questions. It was now about 5 p.m. Attlee communicated our resolution on the telephone. Then they left. When they reached London, Chamberlain had already resigned, and Attlee and Greenwood were asked to go to the Admiralty to see Churchill. It is thus

[26] The National Executive Committee (NEC), the leading executive authority within the Labour party.

clear that the last blow which dislodged the old limpet was struck by us at Bournemouth this afternoon.

Pimlott (ed.), *Political Diary of Hugh Dalton*: entry for 10 May 1940, pp. 344–5.

1.21 Chamberlain's resignation: Churchill becomes Prime Minister

The decision as to whether Chamberlain would be replaced by Churchill or Lord Halifax had already been taken at a highly charged meeting between the three men. Churchill's own account, written later as part of his history of the war, demonstrates his determination to prevail.

At eleven o'clock I was again summoned to Downing Street by the Prime Minister. There once more I found Lord Halifax. We took our seats at the table opposite Mr. Chamberlain. He told us that he was satisfied that it was beyond his power to form a National Government. . . . The question therefore was whom he should advise the King to send for after his own resignation had been accepted. His demeanour was cool, unruffled, and seemingly quite detached from the personal aspect of the affair. He looked at us both across the table.

I have had many important interviews in my public life, and this was certainly the most important. Usually I talk a great deal, but on this occasion I was silent. Mr. Chamberlain evidently had in his mind the stormy scene in the House of Commons two nights before, when I had seemed to be in such heated controversy with the Labour Party. Although this had been in his support and defence, he nevertheless felt that it might be an obstacle to my obtaining their adherence at this juncture. . . . His biographer, Mr. Feiling, states definitely that he preferred Lord Halifax. As I remained silent a very long pause ensued. It certainly seemed longer than the two minutes which one observes in the commemorations of Armistice Day. Then at length Halifax spoke. He said that he felt that his position as a Peer, out of the House of Commons, would make it very difficult for him to discharge the duties of Prime Minister in a war like this. He would be held responsible for everything, but would not have the power to guide the assembly upon whose confidence the life of every Government depended. He spoke for some minutes in this sense, and by the time he had finished it was clear that the duty would fall upon me – had in fact fallen upon me. Then for the first time I spoke. I said I would have no communication with either of the Opposition parties until I had the King's Commission to form a Government. On this the momentous conversation came to an end, and we reverted to our ordinary easy and familiar manners of men who had worked for years together and whose lives in and out of office had been spent in all the friendliness of British politics. . . .

During these last crowded days of the political crisis my pulse had not quickened at any moment. I took it all as it came. But I cannot conceal from the reader of this truthful account that as I went to bed at about 3 a.m. I was conscious of a profound sense of relief. At last I had the authority to give directions over the whole scene. I felt as if I were walking with destiny, and that all my past life had been but a preparation for this hour and for this trial.

Winston S. Churchill, *The Second World War*, Volume 1, *The Gathering Storm*, London, 1948, pp. 597–601.

1.22 Churchill as war leader: the view of Tory loyalists

Churchill's triumph was greeted with dismay by many at Westminster and in Whitehall. The diary of John Colville, Chamberlain's personal secretary, shows that strenous efforts had been made to sway Lord Halifax, who was seen by orthodox Tories as a much safer option than Churchill.

This afternoon we all . . . sat discussing the future form of the Government and weighing the unlikely chance of the King, who (remembering perhaps the Abdication) is understood not to wish to send for Winston, being able to persuade Halifax to recant his determination not to be P.M. We awaited the decision of the Labour Party, who, it was feared, might refuse to serve in any Government of which the P.M. was even a member. At about 4.45 Attlee rang up to say that they would agree to join a Government provided Neville Chamberlain was not P.M.; so now David's[27] idea is that he should

[27] David Margesson, the Chief Whip.

lead the House, as Lord President, like Bonar Law in the last war, while Winston is the new Lloyd George. Provided the P.M. and Halifax remain in the War Cabinet there will at least be some restraint on our new War Lord. He may, of course, be the man of drive and energy the country believes him to be and he may be able to speed up our creaking military and industrial machinery; but it is a terrible risk, it involves the danger of rash and spectacular exploits, and I cannot help fearing that this country may be manoeuvred into the most dangerous position it has ever been in. One thing, however, is certain: if Winston thought the P.M. were trying to hold on to the reins of power he would create such mischief in the House of Commons that a really serious crisis would arise. Nothing can stop him having his way – because of his powers of blackmail – unless the King makes full use of his prerogative and sends for another man; unfortunately there is only one other, the unpersuadable Halifax. . . .

7.05 p.m.: The P.M. has come back from the Palace. Ministers not in the Cabinet have been sent for and told they will have to resign. The King has sent for Winston (fortunately, because Halifax, true to form, had gone off to the dentist!).

7.15: Alec [Dunglass] and I went over to the F[oreign] O[ffice] to explain the position to Rab, and there, with Chips, we drank in champagne the health of the 'King over the Water' (not King Leopold,[28] but Mr Chamberlain). Rab said he thought that the good clean tradition of English politics, that of Pitt as opposed to Fox, had been sold to the greatest adventurer of modern political history. He had tried earnestly and long to persuade Halifax to accept the Premiership, but he had failed. He believed this sudden coup of Winston and his rabble was a serious disaster and an unnecessary one: the 'pass had been sold' by Mr C., Lord Halifax and Oliver Stanley.[29] They had weakly surrendered to a half-breed American. . . .

John Colville, *The Fringes of Power. Downing Street Diaries 1939-1955* London, 1985: diary entry for 10 May 1940, pp. 121–2.

[28] King Leopold of Belgium, who assumed control of Belgian forces but subsequently surrendered to the Germans.

[29] Secretary of State for War, and another of Chamberlain's senior allies during the 1930s.

2

Churchill and Britain's 'finest hour'

Winston Churchill came to power at a time of grave national crisis. German forces rapidly overran the Low Countries in May 1940, forcing a desperate British evacuation from Dunkirk. In the weeks that followed, the collapse of France meant that Britain faced imminent invasion, a threat that only receded after the RAF heroically denied the Germans air supremacy. As this chapter shows, Churchill not only had to rally the nation in order to 'stand alone', he also had to convince many doubters about his suitability for the premiership. In spite of scepticism – especially among Conservatives dismayed by the fall of Chamberlain and the formation of a coalition with Labour – the new Prime Minister quickly exerted his authority. By the end of 1940, with British citizens enduring the horrors of the Blitz, Churchill had established himself as an unrivalled war leader.

2.1 Forming the new coalition

Churchill's first task as Prime Minister was to construct a new government that would include both Conservative and Labour members. His efforts were complicated by the question of what position to offer Chamberlain, who still remained leader of the Conservative party.

Clem Davies came round after lunch to tell me that Attlee and Greenwood had had a long interview in the morning with Winston and had expostulated strongly against the proposal that Neville should be Chancellor and leader of the House and that he thought that they had shaken Winston considerably. Was it possible that I could do anything to shake him further before they saw him again at four o'clock?. . . . Bobbety Cranborne[1] rang me up to ask what was happening. I told him and also had a few words with his father, and urged Salisbury to ring up Winston at the Admiralty at once and convey our views, especially against the idea of Neville being Chancellor of the Exchequer. Salisbury promised to do so and I believe what he said made all the difference. For when the Labour leaders met Winston again he was ready to agree that Neville should be neither Chancellor of the Exchequer nor leader of the House, which latter post he was prepared to take himself though with Neville as deputy. Even this the Labour leaders were doubtful about but were not prepared to quarrel over and the matter is at present in abeyance. Neville of course will remain leader of the Party as Asquith did in December 1916, but that need not cause difficulties. . . .

It was not till nine o'clock that the wireless informed us that the War Cabinet was to consist of only five, Winston, Neville, Halifax, Greenwood and Attlee. The last two were a change upon the original idea of Greenwood and Bevin[2] and Clem thinks that Bevin may be angry and make trouble. . . . Other appointments so far are: Eden to War Office, Alexander to Admiralty, and Sinclair to Air Ministry, Winston keeping defence as a whole in his own hands. How Winston thinks he can be Prime Minister, co-ordinator of defence and leader of the House all in one, is puzzling, and confirms my belief that he really means the present arrangement to be temporary. . . . Rang up Cranborne and heard that he and his father were coming up to town tomorrow to lunch with Winston which would give a further opportunity of pressing the necessity for proper regard for the views of the younger Conservatives who, after all, decided the issue, particularly with regard to the elimination of Margesson.[3]

Barnes and Nicholson (eds), *Amery Diary*: entry for 11 May 1940, pp. 614–15.

[1] Robert Gascoyne-Cecil, Viscount Cranborne, son and heir of the Tory statesman Lord Salisbury.

[2] Ernest Bevin, General Secretary of the Transport and General Workers' Union, who was invited to join the coalition as Minister of Labour in order to symbolise Churchill's willingness to work more closely with the trade unions.

[3] In the event Margesson remained in office as Secretary of State for War. Chamberlain was eventually appointed Lord President of the Council, a post which left him with considerable authority on the home front.

2.2 The new Prime Minister meets the House of Commons

Although the coalition was overwhelmingly endorsed by parliament, Chamberlainites in the Conservative party were clearly disturbed by the sight of both Churchill as Prime Minister and Labour on the government benches.

The House today was absurdly dramatic and very Winstonian: first of all we were summoned by a telegram signed by the Speaker, and asked not to mention the meeting. But as both Houses were summoned, over 1300 telegrams must have been sent, and must have been seen by literally thousands of people. . . .

I was surprised as I thought W[inston] C[hurchill] would have a triumph, at least today, but he very definitely did not. After Prayers he went into the Chamber and was greeted with some cheers but when, a moment later, Neville entered with his usual shy retiring little manner, MPs lost their heads; they shouted; they cheered; they waved their Order Papers, and his reception was a regular ovation. The new PM spoke well, even dramatically, in support of the new all-Party Government, but he was not well received. And all the speeches that followed were mediocre. Only references to Neville raised enthusiasm. . . .

There was some amusement, too, over the seating quandary. If there was to be no Opposition, who would sit in the Opposition benches? Wedgwood, mad as your hat, attempted to proclaim himself a sort of leader of an official Opposition and sat in Mr Attlee's late place – that little gad-fly looked smaller and more insignificant than ever on the Government Front Bench, dwarfed by Winston.

Rhodes James (ed.), *Channon Diary*: entry for 13 May 1940, p. 252.

2.3 Dunkirk and the debate about continuing the war

The new government was powerless to prevent Hitler's forces from overruning the Low Countries, forcing British troops to beat a hasty retreat towards Dunkirk. John Colville – surprised to find that his loyalty to Chamberlain did not prevent him continuing as private secretary at Downing Street – noted how this led to intense discussions about Britain's prospects.

At Downing Street I was distressed to find the situation much blacker than when I left on Friday. It appears that a grave deterioration has taken place in the last forty-eight hours: the B[ritish] E[xpeditionary] F[orce], unable to force their way southwards, have got to retreat to the coast as best they can and re-embark for England from whatever Channel ports remain open to them. The French seem to be demoralised and there is now a serious fear that they may collapse. The Cabinet are feverishly considering our ability to carry on the war alone in such circumstances, and there are signs that Halifax is being defeatist. He says that our aim can no longer be to crush Germany but rather to preserve our own integrity and independence. . . .

There was a Cabinet at 10.00 p.m. to discuss the situation caused by King Leopold's determination, despite the opposition of his Government on English soil, to ask for an armistice. This defection of the Belgians leaves the B.E.F. in an exposed and extremely dangerous position. Duff Cooper told me he was afraid 'a lot of them will be scuppered'.

After the Cabinet I went over to Admiralty House with the P.M. He said he did not think the French would give in and that at any rate they ought not to do so. At midnight, after reading a few papers and saying 'Pour me out a whisky and soda, very weak, there's a good boy', he went to bed.

Colville, *Fringes of Power*: entry for 27 May 1940, pp. 140–1.

2.4 Churchill rallies the government

Although privately alarmed by Britain's worsening military plight, Churchill was soon impressing his new ministerial colleagues with his bulldog determination to fight on at whatever cost.

In the afternoon all ministers are asked to meet the P.M. He is quite magnificent. The man, and the only man we have, for this hour. He gives a full, frank and completely calm account of events in France. When the Germans broke through on the Meuse, French morale for the moment collapsed. . . . Only Dunkirk was left to us. Calais had been defended by a British force which had refused to surrender, and it was said that there were no survivors. We could only use the beaches east and west of Dunkirk in addition to the port itself. Dunkirk was under a pall of black smoke, to which our ships were adding artificial smoke so as to screen our embarkations from the air. . . .

He was determined to prepare public opinion for bad tidings, and it would of course be said, and with some truth, that what was now happening in Northern France would be the greatest British military defeat for many centuries. We must now prepare for the sudden turning of the war against this island, and prepare also for other events of great gravity in Europe. No countenance should be given publicly to the view that France might soon collapse, but we must not allow ourselves to be taken by surprise by any events. . . .

It was idle to think that, if we tried to make peace now, we should get better terms from Germany than if we went on and fought it out. The Germans would demand our fleet – that would be called 'disarmament' – our naval bases and much else. We should become a slave state, though a British government which would be Hitler's puppet would be set up – 'under Mosley[4] or some such person'. And where should we be at the end of all that? On the other side, we had immense reserves and advantages. Therefore, he said, 'We shall go on and we shall fight it out, here or elsewhere, and if at last the long story is to end, it were better it should end, not through surrender, but only when we are rolling senseless on the ground'. There was a murmur of approval round the table, in which I think Amery, Lord Lloyd[5] and I were loudest. Not much more was said. No one expressed even the faintest flicker of dissent. . . . It is clear that whereas the Old Umbrella[6] – neither he nor other members of the War Cabinet were present – wanted to run early, Winston's bias is all the other way.

B. Pimlott, *The Second World War Diary of Hugh Dalton*, London, 1986: entry for 28 May 1940, pp. 26–9.

2.5 Churchill rallies the nation

In parliament the Prime Minister also began to establish his

[4] Oswald Mosley, leader of the British Union of Fascists.
[5] George Lloyd, Colonial Secretary and Conservative leader of the House of Lords.
[6] Dalton's scathing term for Neville Chamberlain.

reputation with a series of defiant speeches. His pledge to 'fight on the beaches' if necessary moved even some of his fiercest former critics.

The Prime Minister made an important and moving statement. I sat behind him (he was next to Neville who looked tiny and fragile), and he was eloquent, and oratorical, and used magnificent English; several Labour Members cried. He hinted that we might be obliged to fight alone, without France, and that England might well be invaded. How the atmosphere has changed from only a few weeks ago when idiotic MPs were talking academic nonsense about our restoring independence to Warsaw and Prague.

Jock Colville tells me that the Admiralty is fantastic now; people who were at each other's throats a few weeks ago are now intimate and on the best of terms. Winston darts in and out, a mountain of energy and good-nature, the Labour leaders, Brendan Bracken and Prof. Lindemann, sometimes Randolph, Beaverbrook, the Defence Ministers, etc. – the new racket all much in evidence, but no Neville and no Horace Wilson.[7]

Rhodes James (ed.), *Channon Diary*: entry for 4 June 1940, p. 256.

2.6 The attack on the appeasers

Churchill's task in coping with Dunkirk and the imminent collapse of France was complicated by a desire to find scapegoats. The obvious targets were ministers associated with appeasement, still serving in the coalition, but now pilloried in various quarters, notably in a best-selling booklet published by three journalists, one of whom was Michael Foot.

How was it, you may ask, that the bravest sons of Britain ever came to be placed in such jeopardy? Yes, well may you ask it. How was it, that, though the best soldiers in the world, they were driven back from Belgium? How was it that on the men along the roads of Belgium and even amid the sand dunes the German airmen seemed

[7] Aside from Brendan Bracken, three key figures in Churchill's entourage were his son, Randolph, the newspaper proprietor Lord Beaverbrook (now Minister of Aircraft Production) and Frederick Lindemann, an Oxford don.

able to work their will as they pleased? How was it that in the last resort their safety depended not on their unmatched skill with weapons, not on their doubtless heroism, not on their unbroken discipline, but partly too on a calm sea, shallow waters and one miraculously immune pierhead?

We know the various, complicated answers. The bridges on the Meuse that were not blown up, the treacherous King of the Belgians, the mistaken notions of defensive war – all these and many more played their part. But there is another answer more truthful and more comprehensive. It was the answer stuttered by every soldier as he stepped ashore. . . . 'Give us the same equipment as the Germans, and we will finish them in three months'. That is the right answer. Men against machines. . . . Here then in three words is the story. Flesh against steel. The flesh of heroes, but none the less, flesh. It is the story of an Army doomed before they took the field. . . .

On May 10th the Chamberlain government fell, and Mr Churchill took power. A new determination at once broke through. Already, and at long last, the aeroplanes, the tanks, the arms of every kind are piling up. . . . But one final and absolute guarantee is still imperatively demanded by a people determined to resist and conquer: namely, that the men who are now repairing the breaches in our walls should not carry along with them those who let the walls fall into ruin. The nation is united to a man in its desire to prosecute the war in total form: there must be a similar unity in the national confidence. Let the guilty men retire, then, of their own volition, and so make an essential contribution to the victory upon which we are implacably resolved.

'Cato', *Guilty Men*, London, 1940, pp. 14 and 124–5.

2.7 Churchill defends the 'men of Munich'

The Prime Minister, lacking a solid party base of his own, believed he had no choice but to defend Chamberlain, as he explained on 7 June to Cecil King, director of one of the most critical newspapers, the *Daily Mirror*.

Churchill said that he had only been Prime Minister for a month and already the papers were picking on the government and demanding

Chamberlain's head on a charger. He thought the debate on Tuesday would amount to nothing; if there was any serious criticism he would take a vote of confidence and no more than 20 would vote against him. He went on that there was no one in the government he had had to accept, but he was glad to have Neville Chamberlain – 'the best man he had' – unlike some of the others who were mediocre. . . .

Churchill said not to forget that a year ago last Christmas they were trying to hound him out of his constituency. . . . But the men who supported Chamberlain and hounded Churchill were still MPs. A General Election was not possible during a war so the present House of Commons, however unrepresentative of feeling in the country, had to be reckoned with as the ultimate source of power for the duration. If Churchill trampled on these men, as he could trample on them, they would set themselves against him, and in such internecine strife lay the Germans' best chance of victory. It was all very well to plead for the government to exclude those who had led us astray, but where would this stop? They were everywhere in politics, the civil service and the military. . . . No, he was not going to run a government of revenge.

Hugh Cudlipp, *Publish and Be Damned! The Astonishing Story of the Daily Mirror*, London, 1953, pp. 144–5.

2.8 The Lloyd George problem

Chamberlain had hitherto resisted the idea that a coalition post should be offered to his long-standing enemy, Lloyd George. Churchill, fearing that Lloyd George would become the focus for opposition among those who anticipated British defeat, was now able to override Chamberlain's resistance, but without being able to entice Lloyd George into government.

14 June The other day L[loyd] G[eorge] received a firm and definite offer to go into the Cabinet from Winston, Neville Chamberlain having concurred in the suggestion. I was against L.G. going in at the time he wrote to Winston, but now the situation has deteriorated so much that it is vital that L.G. should be inside. He has such a vision, and I have such faith in him still. Beaverbrook has been trying to induce L.G. to accept. Frances and I[8] have both impressed upon him the importance of his accepting. But he now sticks his toes in and says: 'I won't go in with this crowd', which means Neville.

27 June . . . He so hates Neville that he would almost rather see the country go the dogs, so that he could point his finger at Neville and say: 'That is the fellow who is responsible'. That is the view of Frances. He sought consolation in impressing upon me that Wales held out centuries ago, even when England was invaded.

C. Cross (ed.), *Life with Lloyd George. The Diary of A. J. Sylvester 1931–45*, London, 1975: entries for 14 and 27 June 1940, pp. 267–70.

2.9 The under-secretaries 'plot'

With France on the point of surrender, Churchill also had to face discontent from within the ranks of his own administration. As Leo Amery here notes, several junior ministers felt that there must be a clean break and dramatic measures introduced to galvanise the government machine.

Walter Monckton[9] to lunch. . . . He told me that the Ministry of Information were receiving from all over the country signs of strong feeling against Neville and the 'Old Gang'. Saw [Churchill] for a moment afterwards and asked when he would give me a few minutes. He pleaded pressure of time and suggested my writing and seeing him later. . . . Back to the office and just as I was starting writing to W[inston] I got a message saying he could see me after all.

I began by setting out the view of my junior colleagues as to making the wheels of administration move faster and making the members of the War Cabinet really masters of their groups of departments. He then said that Neville had told him that this was all an intrigue by George Lloyd and myself to get the Cabinet changed. I protested, pointing out that George at any rate had not discussed these matters with the others, and that both he and I were

[8] Frances Stevenson, Lloyd George's mistress for many years before becoming his second wife. A. J. Sylvester was secretary to the former Prime Minister.

[9] Monckton was Director-General of the Ministry of Information, established to co-ordinate propaganda and monitor the nation's morale.

wholeheartedly interested in the work of our departments and wanted nothing else. As for the juniors they were in direct contact with the working of the machine and greatly concerned with the urgency and dangers of the situation and quite entitled to convey their views. W. differed, thinking their business was to stick to the job he had given them. If any one of the Government wished to criticise its working or its composition they should resign and criticise from outside. He was going to make no changes of any kind and would sooner resign himself than be pressed to do so; I repeated that so far as I was concerned I wanted no other work than I was doing. There was a good deal else, not directly relevant, and we ended in friendly fashion.

But my instinctive doubts about the urgency of the juniors proved right. However desperate the national crisis may be men cannot help thinking of themselves and Clem, Boothby, etc. had successfully frightened Attlee, Greenwood and above all Neville and roused Winston's authoritarian instincts. They had better resign themselves for the time being to doing their work, however acute their sense of national danger.

Barnes and Nicholson (eds), *Amery Diary*: entry for 18 June 1940, pp. 625–6.

2.10 Churchill's 'finest hour' speech

On the same day as he squashed the 'under-secretaries plot', Churchill made perhaps his best-known speech in the House of Commons, which began by repeating that he would not tolerate recriminations at a time of national emergency.

We have to think of the future and not of the past. This also applies in a small way to our own affairs at home. There are many who would hold an inquest in the House of Commons on the conduct of the Governments . . . during the years which led up to this catastrophe. They seek to indict those who were responsible for the guidance of our affairs. This also would be a foolish and pernicious process. There are too many in it. Let each man search his conscience and search his speeches. I frequently search mine. . . .

The disastrous military events which have happened during the past fortnight have not come to me with any sense of surprise. Indeed, I indicated a fortnight ago as clearly as I could to the House that the worst possibilities were open; and I made it perfectly clear then that whatever happened in France would make no difference to the resolve of Britain and the British Empire to fight on, 'if necessary for years, if necessary alone'. During the last few days we have successfully brought off the great majority of the troops we had on the lines of communication in France; and seven-eighths of the troops we have sent to France since the beginning of the war – that is to say, about 350,000 out of 400,000 men – are safely back in this country. . . .

What General Weygand called the Battle of France is over. I expect that the Battle of Britain is about to begin. Upon this battle depends the survival of Christian civilisation. Upon it depends our own British life, and the long continuity of our institutions and our Empire. The whole fury and might of the enemy must very soon be turned on us. Hitler knows that he will have to break us in this island or lose the war. If we can stand up to him, all Europe may be free and the life of the world may move forward into broad, sunlit uplands. But if we fail, then the whole world, including the United States, including all that we have known and cared for, will sink into the abyss of a new Dark Age made more sinister, and perhaps more protracted, by the lights of perverted science. Let us therefore brace ourselves to our duties, and so bear ourselves that, if the British Empire and its Commonwealth last for a thousand years, men will still say, 'This was their finest hour'.

C. Eade (ed.), *The War Speeches of the Rt. Hon. Winston S. Churchill*, Vol. 1, London, 1951, pp. 198–9 and 206–7.

2.11 Reaction to Churchill's speech

In listening to the Prime Minister's famous oration, Hugh Dalton from the Labour side noted that Conservative MPs – instinctively loyalty to Chamberlain as party leader – were still reserved in their attitude.

House of Commons. Winston again makes a grand speech – defiant, reasoned, and confident. It is noticeable that he is much more loudly cheered by the Labour Party than by the general body of Tory supporters. The relative silence of these latter is regarded by some as 'sinister'. John Wilmot,[10] whom I ask to feel about and ascertain opinion, tells me that many Tories feel they are quite out of it now. They think the Labour Party has much too large a share, both in offices and the determination of Government policy, and in addition to being a large part of the Government, the Labour Party also continues to be, to a great extent, the Opposition, so far as status is concerned. The Tories, therefore, wonder where they come in. Most of the Tories in the Government are either rebels or near-rebels. So what was the use of having been loyal to the Old Man and Margesson in the now closed chapter of our history?[11] There is some danger in this situation, and it must be watched. One very obvious conclusion is that we must not push the Old Man out of the Government, for he would then become a centre of disaffection and a rallying point for real opposition. Leave him where he is, as a decaying hostage.

Pimlott (ed.), *Second World War Diary of Hugh Dalton*: entry for 18 June 1940, p. 42.

2.12 Churchill ascendant as war leader

Only in early July, with a German invasion staring Britain in the face, did Conservative MPs finally relent to give the new Prime Minister a more enthusiastic welcome. According to Paul Einzig, a financial journalist working in London, the impetus for a change of attitude came after Neville Chamberlain was persuaded that events in the Commons were creating a poor impression in the United States.

For nearly two months after the advent of Churchill the overwhelming majority of Tory backbenchers, whatever their inner feelings may have been, gave no outward evidence of their support for him. Indeed on many occasions they went out of their way to demonstrate their unwillingness to do so. There was strong resentment amongst them over the appointment of some Tory 'rebels' – looked upon as

[10] John Wilmot, Labour MP for Kennington and Dalton's PPS.
[11] The Old Man was another of Dalton's terms for Chamberlain.

'traitors' by orthodox Tories – to Ministerial posts, and over the removal of a number of loyal Chamberlainite Ministers to make room for these 'rebels' and for representatives of the other parties taking part in the Coalition. Most Conservative Members felt, moreover, that any demonstration of their support to the new Prime Minister would be disloyal to his predecessor owing to the circumstances in which the change of Government came about in May 1940.

One would have thought that during the critical weeks before and immediately after Dunkirk there were more important things to worry about. But, human nature being what it is, such considerations did influence the attitude of hundreds of backbenchers. They demonstrated their resentment by their sullen silence whenever Churchill entered the Chamber or rose to make a speech. . . .

To observers from the galleries this must have conveyed the impression that Churchill's supporters consisted almost exclusively of Members of the former Opposition, representing a small minority of the House. . . . These impressions were bound to influence the attitude of the United States Government when trying to make up its mind whether to continue to supply arms to Britain. Many influential Americans came to the conclusion that the Tory majority was not behind Churchill in his determination to fight against heavy odds. . . .

I came to the conclusion that there was only one man who would be in a position to induce the Tory backbenchers to change their attitude – Neville Chamberlain. After relinquishing the Premiership he remained Leader of the Conservative Party, and the overwhelming majority of the rank and file stood solidly behind him. I was convinced that a word from him to his supporters would make all the difference. Accordingly at the end of June I decided to approach him about this difficult and delicate matter. . . .

He took my frankness in the right spirit and repeatedly emphasised his appreciation of my motives in writing to him. So far, so good. But he flatly rejected my argument, calling in question my interpretation of the scenes I had witnessed in the Chamber. And, although his explanation of the passive attitude of Tory backbenchers did credit to his loyalty to his supporters, to me it did not sound convincing or helpful. . . .

What could Chamberlain have meant, I wondered, by undertaking to see that my impression concerning the demeanour of Tory backbenchers was not confirmed by 'something more serious'?. . . .

Two days later, on July 4, I was told on my arrival at the House that the Prime Minister would make a statement of first-rate importance at 3.30 p.m. . . . It was one of Churchill's greatest speeches, giving an account of the destruction of the French fleet at Oran. . . . My pessimism appeared to receive full confirmation when Churchill sat down after concluding his speech. For, while all Socialists facing him rose at once to a man and cheered him loudly, the Tories remained seated and silent. . . .

Suddenly, however, something remarkable happened. The Chief Conservative Whip, Margesson, rose to his feet. Turning towards the Tory backbenchers, he waved his Order Papers in a gesture clearly conveying instructions that they too should rise. At this signal all the Conservatives, behind the Treasury bench and below the gangway on both sides of the Chamber, rose to a man and burst into enthusiastic cheering at the top of their voices. . . .

Margesson's signal brought their conflict of loyalties to an end. It was evidently a great relief for most of them to be able now to cheer Churchill without feeling that in doing so they might hurt Chamberlain.

Paul Einzig, *In the Centre of Things*, London, 1960, pp. 209–19.

2.13 Coalition politics: the Tories on the defensive

The ambivalence of Conservative MPs towards Churchill was symptomatic of how far the party had been shaken by events since May 1940. As this diary extract of a backbencher illustrates, it was particularly difficult coming to terms with Labour's sudden upturn in political fortune.

There was a debate in the H[ouse] of C[ommons] on the defence regulations to which I cannot say I listened very much. It was mainly conducted (as all debates now are) by the Labour Party – it is odd how the Conservatives, even the stock bores who usually keep talking, have passed out of the picture. I am told that many of the best of them are now away with the forces and of course some of them are not – and never were – talkers. No doubt, too, those who might intervene in debate more often feel, as I do, that there is no object in making speeches nowadays, all the same, I feel that we are mistaken and ought not to allow the Socialists such a free run. There is of course 'a party truce', but it is only observed by one side. Every speech made by the Labour people in the H[ouse] of C[ommons] is a party speech and is propaganda. Of course our side ought to organise itself and arrangements should be made for certain MPs to speak in all important debates to put forward the Conservative view. The trouble is that Winston appears to be the only man to lead us and he is quite incapable of the job. There are some other ex-cabinet ministers . . . but not only are they masquerading as soldiers but they are also, none of them, suitable men to lead a party. It is altogether a bad look out for the future and it looks as if everything we ought to stand for will go by default.

S. Ball (ed.), *Parliament and Politics in the age of Churchill and Attlee: The Headlam Diaries 1934–51*, London, forthcoming: entry for 31 July 1940.

2.14 The invasion threat

By mid-summer in 1940, the main preoccupation of politicians, as for the nation in general, was the threat of a Nazi invasion, now expected at any moment.

I think that Hitler will probably invade us within the next few days. He has 6,000 aeroplanes ready for the job. How strange it all is! We know that we are faced with a terrific invasion. We half-know that the odds are heavily against us. Yet there is a sort of exhilaration in the air. If Hitler were to postpone invasion and fiddle about in Africa or the Mediterranean, our morale might weaken. But we are really proud to be the people who will not give way. The reaction to Hitler's speech yesterday is a good reaction. Yet I know well that we shall be exposed to horrible punishment. It is so strange that in this moment of anxiety there is no hatred of Hitler or the Germans. Opinion slides off into oblique animosities such as criticism of the Old Gang and rage that the L[ocal] D[efence] V[olunteers] are not better equipped.[12] All this is dangerous, since it is in essence a form of

[12] The Old Gang came into wide usage as a means of referring to Chamberlain and the so-called 'men of Munich'. LDV was the name initially used for the Home Guard.

escapism and appeasement. We are really frightened of Hitler, and avoid the dynamic resistance to him which is uniform hatred. One hundred and thirty years ago all this hatred was concentrated against Bonaparte. We flinch today from central enmity. If we are invaded we may become angry.

Nicolson (ed.), *Harold Nicolson Diary*: entry for 20 July 1940, pp. 103–4.

2.15 The Battle of Britain

If Hitler was to invade, the Germans first needed to establish air supremacy over Britain. As Churchill's secretary noted, the famous aerial encounters of the Battle of Britain were never far from the Prime Minister's mind, even when entertaining ministerial colleagues at Chequers.

Beaverbrook and Bevin arrived, and I dined alone with them and Winston. Grouse has been specially ordered, it having become legal to shoot them on August 5th this year. . . . During dinner it was amusing to hear Beaverbrook flatter Bevin, calling him a natural House of Commons man and saying that he was the only orator in the Labour Party. Bevin said the war would be won in the Middle East and it was essential, for the sake of morale in this country, to deal the Italians a resounding blow. One was enough; after that they would collapse. Beaverbrook said he thought morale in this country was all right, and when we received set-backs we braced ourselves the more. Bevin was doubtful and considered that success was sorely needed. I wondered who knew best, the newspaper magnate or the Labour leader. I am inclined to think the latter. . . .

The Prime Minister asked me to come and talk to him while he was undressing and was most genial. He said Bevin was a good old thing and had 'the right stuff in him' – no defeatist tendencies. He expatiated on the debt we owed to our airmen and claimed that the life of the country depended on their intrepid spirit. What a slender thread, he exclaimed, his voice tremulous with emotion, the greatest of things can hang by! He has cause to be elated: today our fighters accounted for about seventy German planes over the Channel.

Colville, *Fringes of Power*: entry for 11 August 1940, pp. 219–20.

2.16 Lord Beaverbrook and cabinet changes

In this interview with Britain's Air Minister, the editor of the *Manchester Guardian* discovers that Chamberlain would not be a political force for much longer, and that party considerations were still important in determining promotion to the War Cabinet.

12 Noon. Lord Beaverbrook at Imperial Chemicals House
'Come outside, Mr Crozier', said Beaverbrook and led the way to the balcony, where he leaned on the railing looking out on the Embankment Gardens. 'It's the curse of my life', he said, 'having to talk to these Air Marshals for an hour or two hours every morning. . . . I'd like to get back to newspaper work'. . . .

'Well, perhaps you will before long'.

'Why, do you think they're going to kick me out?'

'No, but people say so much about your performing miracles in producing aircraft that I thought you might have some more up your sleeve. But, seriously, what does your being in the War Cabinet mean?. . . .

Then he went on – 'I don't want to go into the War Cabinet. But as soon as I started getting some success with this production business Churchill began to put one piece of work on me after another, until at last he wanted to bring me into the War Cabinet. And when I said I didn't want to go in he said that no one would ever do what he wanted, and so I had to give way.'

'Well', I said, 'is he going to reconstruct his Ministry? Chamberlain is going, so they say, and perhaps Halifax with him, and in that case there will have to be reconstruction, won't there?'

Beaverbrook 'I don't think there's going to be reconstruction – because I don't think there's anything to reconstruct. Chamberlain – well, he hasn't exactly resigned. . . . he's done, he's finished, you need not reckon with him any more as a force in politics – he's got cancer of the bowels – he's finished – you can wipe him out in politics!'. . . ..

Then he began to describe Churchill's difficulties – 'He wanted to bring Herbert Morrison into the War Cabinet recently. . . . But the Tory "machine" would not let him. The Tory managers, Kingsley Wood, Captain Margesson and others, held a meeting and decided that to have Morrison brought in would disturb the balance of the parties in the War Cabinet and they would not have it. But' – he

raised his voice again – 'they decided that it would be all right for me to be brought in as a Tory, and when I heard that I was regarded as a representative of the Tory party I gave the biggest laugh that has ever been heard', and at this he laughed loudly again and again. 'Well, I'll tell you one thing, Mr Crozier, I'm not nearly such a Conservative as Herbert Morrison!'
Taylor (ed.), *Off the Record*: interview dated 24 August 1940, pp. 196-9.

2.17 Politicians and the Blitz

This extract demonstrates that politicians were just as vulnerable as civilians to aerial bombardment in the Blitz – Hitler's attempt to bomb Britain into submission – though working-class families in the East End were not as fortunate in what might follow the destruction of their homes.

Geoffrey Lloyd, Alan and the Butlers dined, and it was a memorable evening. . . . Sydney Butler's[13] first evening in London since the blitz. Dinner proceeded, and suddenly Lambert, the butler, ushered in what appeared to be a Harlem nigger: it was Harold Balfour,[14] black from head to foot. He had been standing in the smoking room of the Carlton Club with David Margesson...drinking sherry before going into dinner: suddenly, with a blinding flash, the ceiling had fallen in, and the club collapsed on them. A direct hit. Harold swam, as he put it, through the rubble, surprised to be alive, but soon realised that his limbs were all intact: he called out to his companions to see if they were still alive, and fortunately, all answered. Somehow he got to the front door...to find it jammed. At that moment he saw Lord Hailsham being half led, half carried out by his son, Quintin Hogg.[15] A few other individuals, headed by Harold, put their shoulders to the door, and it crashed into the street, and only just in time as by then a fire had started. Harold remembered that he had left his car, an Air Force one, nearby, and went to it, and found only a battered heap of tin; but the chauffeur, an RAF man, was luckily untouched, as he had

[13] Sydney Butler was the wife of the Conservative minister Rab Butler.
[14] Captain Harold Balfour, Tory MP and under-secretary at the Air Ministry.
[15] Like Balfour, Lord Hailsham and his MP son were dining at the Conservative club, the Carlton.

gone into the building. Harold came here for a bath, champagne, and succour, and we gave him all three.

Rhodes James (ed.), *Channon Diary*: entry for 14 October 1940, pp. 269–70.

2.18 Churchill as leader of the Conservative party

As expected, Neville Chamberlain resigned from the government in the autumn, and died shortly afterwards. In his later history of the war, Churchill candidly admitted that it would have been foolish to turn down the chance to succeed Chamberlain as party leader.

At the end of September Mr. Chamberlain's health got far worse. The exploratory operation to which he had subjected himself in July and from which he had returned so courageously to duty had revealed to the doctors that he was suffering from cancer and that there was no surgical remedy. He now became aware of the truth and that he would never be able to return to his work. He therefore placed his resignation in my hands. . . . Sir John Anderson[16] became Lord President of the Council and presided over the Home Affairs Committee of the Cabinet. Mr. Herbert Morrison succeeded him as Home Secretary and Minister of Home Security, and Sir Andrew Duncan became Minister of Supply. These changes were effective on October 3.

Mr. Chamberlain also thought it right to resign the Leadership of the Conservative Party, and I was invited to take his place. I had to ask myself the question . . . whether the Leadership of one great party was compatible with the position I held from King and Parliament as Prime Minister of an Administration composed of, and officially supported by, all parties. I had no doubt about the answer. The Conservative Party possessed a very large majority in the House of Commons over all other parties combined. Owing to the war conditions no election appeal to the nation was available in case of disagreement or deadlock. I should have found it impossible to

[16] Anderson was a leading civil servant between the wars. He had become National MP for the Scottish Universities in 1938 and had been Home Secretary since September 1939.

conduct the war if I had had to procure the agreement in the compulsive days of crisis and during long years of adverse and baffling struggle not only of the Leaders of the two minority parties but of the Leader of the Conservative majority. Whoever had been chosen and whatever his self-denying virtues, he would have had the real political power. For me there would have been only the executive responsibility. . . .

I therefore accepted the position of Leader of the Conservative Party which was pressed upon me. . . . Lord Halifax, who might have been an alternative choice of the party if I had declined, himself proposed the motion, which was unanimously adopted.

Winston S. Churchill, *The Second World War*, Vol. II, *Their Finest Hour*, London, 1949, pp. 438–9.

2.19 **Report on England**

The death of Neville Chamberlain removed any division of loyalty felt by Tory MPs, and confirmed what had been apparent for several months – that Winston Churchill was now politically ascendant. This certainly struck one American journalist writing about his experiences in England during late-1940.

Two days before I left, my appointment with Mr. Churchill came through. He would see me at 11.30 a.m.

I was excited about the prospect of meeting the man on whom so much history depends. . . . Before I flew to London I had felt that the weight of England was too precariously balanced on the health and success of a single man. Now I found it impossible to think of the English ceasing their effort to defeat Hitler regardless of what happened to their Prime Minister and notwithstanding his obviously dictatorial position in the Government. But that did not make me any less curious about what he was like. . . .

My first impression was that Winston Churchill was smaller, rounder, neater, and redder than I imagined from his pictures. His eyebrows, his rusty hair, are thin red. . . . I can't honestly say that I came away very much wiser although all my questions, most of which asked his opinion on various phases of international politics and the probable costs of the war and what he felt about America's relations to it, he appeared to be answering simply and frankly. . . .

Everywhere I went in London people admired his energy, his courage, his singleness of purpose. People said they 'didn't know what Britain would do without him'. He was obviously respected. But few felt he would be Prime Minister after the war. He was simply the right man in the right job at the right time. The time being the time of a desperate war with Britain's enemies. Everyone remarked that he loved his job and that he had risen to his terrific responsibilities brilliantly. Two personal failings only were noted – first that while he could be and was utterly ruthless in letting nothing come ahead of the war effort, he had a weakness toward people who were old friends and associates. He found it very difficult to bring himself to remove them even when he knew they were failing him. The second weakness was . . . his penchant for playing general himself. It was felt that he might be too much of a cavalry officer and have too little of the technical knowledge so important in a technical war. . . .

But I asked everyone who I thought might be interested who would be the next Prime Minister if anything should happen to Winston Churchill. Nobody had any idea.

Ralph Ingersoll, *Report on England*, London, 1941, pp. 152, 159 and 165.

3
The war and the war economy

Although Churchill's reputation seemed secure by the end of 1940, criticism of the government had not altogether ceased. Indeed during 1941–42 anxiety mounted about two related questions: how could the war be won and how could the war economy be improved to help secure victory? In the long-term, the entry of the Soviet Union and the United States into the war during 1941 was to have a profound effect. With the support of major allies, Britain could now look forward to moving from the defensive stalemate of 'standing alone' to the prospect of ultimate victory. But military success was slow in coming. This chapter demonstrates a gradual build-up of frustration as heightened expectations combined with a series of British military setbacks, in the Balkans, the Far East and North Africa. Late in 1942 the tide finally began to turn. In the meantime, however, political opinion once more raised serious questions about Churchill's leadership; for several months, it seemed possible that he might be displaced by an unlikely rival – Sir Stafford Cripps.

3.1 Arsenic and Old Lace

Concern amongst MPs that Britain's economic resources were not being mobilised with sufficient urgency led to some unusual alliances, notably that between the right-wing Conservative Earl Winterton and the left-wing Labour MP Manny Shinwell.

In the winter of 1940 Mr. Shinwell and I had a talk, following one I had had with Mr. Hore-Belisha.[1] All three of us thought that there was both justification and necessity for a joint presentation of views, after prior consultation, on certain aspects of defence, foreign policy and supply. . . . There is clearly need for critical comment at times, alike upon the course of events and the Government's reaction to them. A Government as powerful as the National Government has particular need for such comments, and it is in the nations's interest that it should receive them. We did not seek to form a group in the ordinary parliamentary sense of the term. Indeed, we repelled the help of some whom we thought had ulterior motives – of a personal character – in seeking to work with us. We did not want to be the stepping-stones for anyone's ambitions to overthrow the Government in order to have a place in a new one. . . . Even had we formed ourselves into a large, influential, aggressive group, engaged to press certain important issues upon the attention of His Majesty's Government, Mr. Churchill could not, in logic, have objected; for he was the leader . . . of just such a group, in whose membership I was included, during Mr. Baldwin's Premiership.[2] I think that he accepted our position and aims after some preliminary observations of acerbity to which we replied with equal acerbity. The relationship between Mr. Shinwell and myself was described by Mr. Kingsley Martin of the *New Statesman* as 'Arsenic and Old Lace', the title of a celebrated play of the time. The name stuck. I found it easy to work with Mr. Shinwell, despite our differences on domestic policy; I liked his intelligence and integrity. . . . In private we were each of us attacked by personal and political friends for our alliance, which was alleged to be sinister and unnatural. We were not, in the slightest degree, embarrassed or annoyed by these attacks. The House, as a whole, treated us well, and did not regard our efforts as ignoble or self-seeking.

The alliance virtually arose out of a debate at the end of November on man-power and production. The Government were not in a very happy position, as both Mr. Greenwood and the late Mr. Bevin failed to answer Mr. Shinwell's powerful plea for universal organisation and compulsion where it was necessary. Mr. Shinwell showed

[1] Leslie Hore-Belisha, National Liberal MP for Plymouth Devonport. He had been dismissed as Secretary of State for War by Chamberlain in January 1940.

[2] A reference to Churchill's anti-government stance between 1935 and 1937, when the National government was headed by Chamberlain's predecessor as Conservative leader, Stanley Baldwin.

political courage in making such a speech at the time, though what he advocated was, in effect, afterwards adopted by the Government. . . . There was a good deal of criticism of Mr. Bevin in private following the debate. It was not until the next year that he established his position as a first-rate Minister of Labour in a war-time Government.

Earl Winterton, *Orders of the Day*, London, 1953, pp. 260–1.

3.2 Coalition politics and the war economy

Unease about the war economy spread during the first half of 1941 and caused sniping between the major coalition partners, as these extracts from the diary of Churchill's secretary illustrate.

Tuesday, January 21st . . . the House debated Manpower, Production and Supply. The P.M. sat on the Front Bench, and I in the box, while Bevin read out a long oration. Everybody yawned, and the incorrigible Mr Austin Hopkinson[3] even suggested rudely that to save Mr Bevin trouble the Clerk of the Table should read the speech for him; but the House sat up with a start and gaped when Industrial Registration, to make possible conscription in industries of national importance, was announced. After Bevin had spoken for over an hour, Lord Winterton rose and made an eloquent attack on the Government. He said, with some truth, that there was a danger of our forming a kind of 'Maginot Line Complex' about American help. We must not rely on any but our own efforts. . . .

I lunched . . . at the House, and then . . . went into the box to hear the P. M. wind up the debate. He did so extremely well, explaining his reasons for the new committee machinery (which has been much criticised) with utmost clearness and cogency.[4] The House was entertained by his quips and his mastery of the art of anti-climax. He expounded the little known facts about the slowness of changing from peace to war production and the increased need for manpower,

[3] Independent MP for Mossley.

[4] In an effort to demonstrate greater efficiency, the government vested responsibility for the economic war effort in a Production Executive and an Import Executive; the new system was presided over by Bevin as Minister of Labour.

in industry rather than the forces, as that transfer takes place. He answered the demand for a dictator on the Home Front, to correspond with the Minister of Defence on the military side, by disparaging dictators in general and by pointing out that he could only maintain his ascendancy as Minister of Defence because he was also Prime Minister. In general he welcomed criticism even when, for the sake of emphasis, it parted company with reality.

Wednesday, April 23rd The Home Censorship Report (on letters sent abroad from this country) is for the first time a little bit alarming. It shows a certain amount of discontent. People seem to think that the 'ruling classes' are doing well out of the war – which they certainly are not. There is a good deal of criticism of the Government and a lot of the B. B. C. In particular people seem to be getting sick of the hearty propaganda of the 'Are we downhearted?' kind, sponsored by the Government. Brendan points out that there is bound to be criticism of the Government: its 'honeymoon period' is over and the 'grim realities of marriage' have to be faced.

Thursday, June 19th At the House of Commons Tommy Dugdale[5] lamented to me the first signs of a new class feeling between the two sides of the House. The Tories, conscious of the great sacrifices they are making financially and of the exceedingly high wages being paid to war workers, are cantankerous about the many reports of slackness, absenteeism, etc. , in the factories. The Labour Party resent this criticism and blame the managers and employers for any shortcomings. . . .

Colville, *Fringes of Power*, pp. 339–40, 377 and 401–2.

3.3 The loss of Greece and Crete

Dissatisfaction with the government stemmed, at root, from failings on the battlefield. The loss of Greece and Crete demonstrated that old divisions in the Tory party had not entirely disappeared, with orthodox Chamberlainites venting their frustration on the Foreign Secretary, Anthony Eden.

[5] Conservative MP for Richmond in Yorkshire.

30 April Winston made a statement to the House about the evacuation from Greece: it has been less of a disaster than we feared, for over 45,000 men have got away. The House, while restive, was relieved. Anthony also made a statement reading out a message from the Greek Government agreeing to, indeed suggesting, the withdrawal of our troops. . . .

6 May The first day of the Great Debate: and I wonder will Anthony survive it, or rather would he have survived it had not been for 'our' sudden and unexpected decision last week to support him?[6] He opened the debate with an appallingly bad speech; no cheers greeted him and he gave a dim account of his travels and failures. He sat down amidst complete silence. . . . He was followed by a series of speakers all of whom attacked him and the Government. Maurice Petherick said that he wanted a Panzer Government, not a Pansy Government:[7] the whole debate was acrimonious and rude, rather than particularly damaging. . . .

7 May . . . it is a year ago today that we had the great Norway Debate which brought about the fall of Mr Chamberlain. Today was different; again the Government was attacked but the personal position of the Prime Minister was not in question: Anthony was the victim and he was rattled, even pathetic. . . . Soon after 4 o'clock Winston rose, and never have I heard him in such brilliant (although sometimes irrelevant) form; he was pungent, amusing, cruel, hard-hitting and he lashed out at Lloyd George and Winterton with all his inimitable wit and venom. He was completely at ease and enjoyed himself: a magnificent effort, and he tore his opponents to shreds and captivated the House. When the Division came the figures were 447 to 3. A triumph on paper, but in reality the Government is shaken and both Anthony and Winston know it. . . .

1 June The evacuation of Crete is announced and we are told that over 15,000 men got away in our ships. I doubt whether the defence of the island was even worthwhile. It may have delayed the attacking forces in their downward march but it means also a further decline in our prestige. British Expeditionary Forces are now known as 'Back Every Friday'!

6 June On all sides one hears increasing criticism of Churchill. He is undergoing a noticeable slump in popularity and many of his

[6] In this context 'our' refers to Channon and his Chamberlainite associates.

[7] Petherick was Tory MP for Penryn and Falmouth; his notion of a 'Pansy Government' was a rude comment upon Eden's allegedly effeminate nature.

enemies, long silenced by his personal popularity, are once more vocal. Crete has been a great blow to him.

Rhodes James (ed.), *Channon Diary*, pp. 302–4 and 307.

3.4 The Select Committee on National Expenditure

Churchill's task was made more difficult by criticism from the House of Commons Select Committee on National Expenditure. With access to confidential information denied to most MPs, the Conservative chairman was well placed to note that war production was still well below its full capacity.

We are definitely of the opinion that the country is not getting the production that it should and that it is possible with the labour supply available. In view of the increased number of people in industry and the new factories coming into operation there is, and will be an increasing output, but we very much doubt whether enquiry would not show that the actual production per man, per day, is not falling. The bulk of the people are working well, but there is a distinct element, particularly among the young people, men especially, which is not pulling its weight. These people are responsible mainly for the complaints of slack work and absenteeism, although it is also plain that absenteeism is caused by other factors, such as can be and are dealt with by improved transport facilities and the work of welfare officers.

The Essential Works Order is not working well. It is far too cumbrous in its machinery to begin with and is really only being applied on the one side, in favour of the workers. The position of the employer is almost hopeless; he has lost control of his labour, discipline has largely disappeared and the remedies are impracticable in their operation. Both employers and Trades Unions have stressed the necessity for a much speedier method of dealing with the few delinquents who lower the whole tone of the establishment. We do not believe that the attacks made on the employers as a whole are justified; there may be cases in which action against them is necessary, but, if so, the Ministry of Labour has the power and should exercise it impartially against both employers and employed. At present it is not doing so.

Sir John Wardlaw-Milne[8] to Winston Churchill, 21 June 1941, P[ublic] R[ecord] O[ffice] PREM 4 86/2.

3.5 'The House of Commons is very restive'

Hitler's attack on the Soviet Union in mid-1941 meant that Britain at last had a major ally. Although this relieved some of the pressure of 'standing alone' against Nazism, it did not bring immediate military victories. As a result, Harold Macmillan argued, there was still a need for greater leadership on the home front, especially if it came from Beaverbrook.

The political system is bad.

The House of Commons is very restive.

The Press is hostile.

The reasons are:

1. Our impotence to help Russia by direct military effort causes us to search our hearts again.
2. A sense of lack of grip by the Government on internal questions – labour supply, production policy, etc.
3. The 'old gang' are unpopular. (Halifax, Simon, Kingsley-Wood, E. Brown[9]).

The 'new gang' are largely regarded as failures. (Greenwood, Attlee, Duff Cooper).

The Bureaucratic method of Whitehall is becoming known in wider circles: Government by Committee; the Lord President's elephantine slowness; the difficulty of getting decisions.

4. All the symptons are developing which marked the end of the Asquith coalition (a coalition of parties) and the formation of the Lloyd George coaltion (a coalition of personalities).

But in this case, the second coalition must be under the same leadership.

The Prime Minister's personal position is as high as ever. But he is thought to be let down by his loyalties.

5. The War Front and the Home Front should be divided. We want a leader for all that comes under the Home Front. This must include

[8] Conservative MP for Kidderminster and a persistent critic of Churchill's war leadership.

[9] Ernest Brown, Liberal National MP and Minister of Health 1941–43.

Labour, which with Raw Materials and Machine Capacity forms the Trinity of Production.

6. The leader of the Home Front must in effect be second-in-command to the Prime Minister.

He must be a man of vision and energy.

His 'political' alignments are not considered important by the Public.

There is only one possible choice.

7. If the Prime Minister does nothing, he will ride the immediate storm, but the Government will not last beyond the end of this year or the early part of next.

Harold Macmillan to Lord Beaverbrook, 13 October 1941, reprinted in A. J. P. Taylor, *Beaverbrook*, London, 1972, pp. 494–5.

3.6 Conservative critics challenge the Prime Minister

After the United States finally entered the war, Britain could at last look forward to ultimately prevailing over the Axis powers. But far from bringing short-term improvements, British forces suffered a series of reverses that brought Churchill's leadership itself under threat. By early 1942 the lead in attacking the Prime Minister was being taken by the Chamberlainites who dominated the back-bench 1922 Committee.

18 December [1941] To the House, where we sat in Secret Session. There was continued criticism of the Government, a barrage of questions, bickering and obvious dislike. It was another Narvik night. The Government, as it is, is doomed: I give it a few months. No Government could survive such unpopularity for long. Of course, the Members behaved rather like schoolboys with the Headmaster away and no doubt Winston, on his return, will, as usual, harangue us, and possibly pacify the House once more – for a short time.[10] I want Winston to remain Prime Minister certainly, but he should reconstruct his Government. . . .

9 January [1942] Seventeen MPs dined last night at the Dorchester, collected by Erskine Hill, who sees himself as a sort of

[10] Churchill was absent on an extended visit to the United States.

Lord Younger.[11] Anthony Eden was present, and seemed upset when every MP present told him that the Government was doomed. It was no use, they said, the PM coming back and making one of his magical speeches. This time, it would serve no purpose. The Government must be reformed, and that soon. . . .

20 January At the House the Prime Minister arrived and was given a cheer, though hardly could his welcome be called enthusiastic – civil, perhaps. He looked fat and cross, and when he rose to answer his questions it was obvious that he was disappointed with his reception, and that he had a cold, since his voice was almost husky. Such was the reappearance of the great hero, and I was almost sorry for him. . . . He has announced that he will make a broadcast speech next Tuesday, and the House took his suggestion ungraciously. . . .

21 January Winston bowed to the will of the Members by withdrawing his motion for his speech to be broadcast direct. The feeling of the House was strongly against it; and in deciding not to challenge it, he has acted wisely. It is better to placate Parliament on a small matter than to have a row on a minor issue. The boys – the naughty boys – have won a round.

Rhodes James (ed.), *Channon Diary*, pp. 315–7.

3.7 The threat from Sir Stafford Cripps

A new element in the political equation was that in early 1942 Churchill was faced for the first time since coming to power with a major rival. Stafford Cripps[12] arrived back in Britain from his post as Ambassador in Moscow untainted by any failures of the coalition. By making a series of speeches urging the nation to greater sacrifices in order to win the war, Cripps quickly established himself in the public mind as the man of the moment.

Sir Stafford Cripps is today second only to Mr. Winston Churchill in commanding public confidence and popularity in Britain. This is an extraordinary thing, when you realise that just two months ago,

[11] Alexander Erskine Hill, Tory MP for Edinburgh North and chairman of the 1922 Committee; Lord Younger was a senior party figure between the wars.

[12] Labour/Independent MP for Bristol East and Solicitor-General during the 1929–31 Labour government.

when he landed in England on returning from Russia, the great majority of people had little interest in him, and no idea of what he might or should do next. At that time, on January 23rd, a Mass-Observation study showed only one person in five thinking he ought to join the Cabinet or the Government. An appreciable minority of the British public had not even heard of Sir Stafford Cripps, and did not know who he was. . . .

He brought back with him an aura of success from the most successful country in fighting Germany so far, and he came back as the one British politician who has kept right outside the controversies and difficulties of the past two years of war. By the beginning of February his name had [been] quite widely canvassed in the press for the post of Minister of Production. Quite a large number of people were disappointed when Lord Beaverbrook was given first post, now held by Captain Oliver Lyttelton[13]. . . .

The feeling that Sir Stafford Cripps should have some position in the Government continued to increase, but there was still no very strong or widespread public feeling on the subject until Sunday evening, February 8th. On that evening he gave a postscript to the 9 o'clock BBC news. . . . The effect of Sir Stafford's postscript was sensational – sensational, that is, to the student of the public mind, like myself, who generally expects public reactions to be fairly slow and steady, even sometimes sluggish. There was nothing sluggish about this one. Cripps's broadcast was a knock-out. He said something which many people were feeling, which had not been put so clearly before. He said that we must all do more in the war, every one of us, and do it quick. . . .

Ninety-three per cent of a sample studied by Mass-Observation approved this broadcast, mostly with enthusiasm. . . . Especially admired was his insight and frankness, and the feeling of straightforward kindness and human sympathy in his voice. The austere lawyer of public imagination became, after quarter-of-an-hour on the radio, the friendly counsellor of listeners up and down the country.

From that day on, Sir Stafford had a firm grip on the public, and when 12 days later he was appointed to the War Cabinet, nine persons in ten were really pleased – again an exceptionally high figure of approval of anything. People felt that he would become a

[13] Beaverbrook agreed to be production minister on 4 February, but soon resigned and was replaced by Lyttelton, Conservative MP for Aldershot.

guiding leader on the Home Front, leaving Mr. Churchill freer for the strategical and foreign aspects of the war. . . .

Mass-Observation regularly studies . . . which politicians are most popular, and especially who people favour as the next Prime Minister. For the last three and a half years, every poll has shown Mr. Anthony Eden at the top, except in the period before May 1940, when Mr. Churchill was often the most popular candidate, until he actually became Prime Minister. At the end of the first week in March, we made one of our regular surveys and found that for the first time somebody else surpassed Eden in people's voting – namely Sir Stafford Cripps.

Mass-Observation Typescript Report No. 1166, 'Sir Stafford Cripps', 23 March 1942: Mass-Observation archive, University of Sussex.

3.8 The government reshuffle of February 1942

As news came through of British defeat in Singapore, Churchill felt that further criticism could only be forestalled by reconstructing his government. In spite of acclaim for bringing in Cripps and other new faces, both main coalition partners were concerned that the other was securing party advantage, as these extracts from the diary of a junior Labour minister show.

Friday 20 February This morning's papers announced a new War Cabinet. Greenwood, Kingsley Wood & Beaverbrook have gone.[14] Cripps is brought in as Lord Privy Seal & Leader of the House of Commons, Attlee being designated Deputy P.M. & given the post of Dominions Secy.; Lyttelton, one of Churchill's 'toughs', is being brought in as Minister of State to look after Production; Anderson, Eden & Bevin with the P.M. It is said in one line that Beaverbrook is too ill to continue & in the next that he is going to America to carry on with his job there. . . .

Monday 23 February Clouds still surround Churchill. A victory or two would disperse them but no early victories can be expected. His changes are a steady challenge to the Municheers like Southby &

[14] Greenwood was removed as Minister without Portfolio. Kingsley Wood remained as Chancellor of the Exchequer, but now outside the War Cabinet.

Williams.[15] Who is to replace him I don't see and he will probably fight hard against any efforts on the part of the caucuses to impose their nominees on him. The dropping of Margesson & Greenwood & the reduction in status of Kingsley Wood . . . prove this. . . .

Tuesday 24 February The House was in a sullen mood in which Party feeling showed itself more than I have known since May 1940. When Llewellin[16] rose to answer his first question, the Tories & only the Tories cheered. When Dalton made his bow at the box as President of the Board of Trade the Labour men, & only they, cheered. . . .

I went out to lunch. At the Ministers' table I sat next to the Lord Advocate who said there had evidently been a bad mess at Singapore. We had never lost so many men before . . .

Wednesday 25 February At the Party Meeting today . . . Walker[17] tried to raise the whole question of the changes in the Govt. During the vote of censure debate the P.M. had proved that everything was right, he then promptly proved everything was wrong by sacking 5 Ministers of Cabinet rank. Rhys Davies[18] said there were more to be pole-axed. What was the future of reconstruction?. . . .

Attlee said after last week's meeting he at once told the P.M. we wanted a smaller Cabinet. He had done his best; he would willingly give his job to anyone else. Agreeing to the dropping of Greenwood had been a sad necessity. We could not have a continuing political crisis at home while stupendous military dangers faced us throughout the world. When he tried to get the Labour Party representation, he was told he could only put 100 votes in the lobby. . . . The speech did not carry the Party. Members evidently felt they had been 'had' over the dropping of Greenwood.

At the Board I told the President it had been a bad meeting. There was disaffection over the reduction of the War Cabinet. He said so there was in the Tory Party in whose ranks it was said there was now no orthodox Conservative in the War Cabinet. Churchill was not orthodox; Eden was not liked; Anderson had never called himself a Tory; Lyttelton nobody knew & he was regarded as a city shark!. . . .

[15] Tory MPs for Epsom and Croydon South respectively.

[16] J. J. Llewellin, MP for Uxbridge and newly-appointed as Minister of Aircraft Production.

[17] James Walker, Labour MP for Motherwell.

[18] Labour MP for Westhoughton.

Friday 27 February Among the things the P. said yesterday were . . . that Bracken increased the P.M.'s difficulties by describing the Tory back-bench M.P.s as morons. The staggering fact remained, said the P., that a revolt of the Right had brought about a War Cabinet more to the Left.

K. Jefferys (ed.), *Labour and the Wartime Coalition. From the Diary of James Chuter Ede 1941–45*, London, 1987, pp. 52–60.

3.9 **Riding the political storm**

Writing to his Conservative colleague Samuel Hoare, now serving as Britain's Ambassador in Madrid, Rab Butler reflected on how the recent crisis came about and how – for the time being – it had been resolved.

You will ask: 'Who has been organising the purge, and why was it done?' The background is as follows.

While the Prime Minister was in America, people became more and more disquieted about the absence of the Dictator who was, in fact, running the war. They began to ask how decisions could be taken about Singapore by a man who sitting, busily occupied, in Washington. They were not convinced by the presence of Attlee in the Chair of the Defence Committee.

This coincided with a curious inverted conscience on the part of the Private Members of the Conservative Party. These saw things going very badly for the country and their own interest, and they have expressed it to me. They began to search their conscience as to whether they had told the truth to Chamberlain. They came to the conclusion that they hadn't and that they must therefore tell the truth to Churchill. There was nobody to give them good advice about politics.

With this in mind, picture the Prime Minister coming back, piloting his own aeroplane, saying to his friends that he has America behind him and that he must have England behind him, and expressing boredom at the intrigues and burdens of the House of Commons.

The result is that the Private Members kick over the traces and are stupid enough to attack the Prime Minister immediately he returns.

This leads to a revulsion against the ordinary Members of the Party on the part of the Prime Minister and his out-spoken, but very often ill-advised, entourage.

Then come the first changes, making Beaverbrook Minister of Production and so on, which savoured exactly of Neville's last changes.

Then comes the fall of Singapore and a feeling in the country that, as the Russian system is proving so successful against the Germans, we must have something of the sort here.

When the P.M. met the House on top of these new events, he mishandled it badly, underestimating the feeling and showing irritation. . . .

At this stage feeling for once became aroused against the P.M. himself. He therefore decided to respond to the request for further changes, and felt he could hit certain Conservative leaders as hard as he hit Labour misfits, such as Greenwood – and I always think Brendan Bracken has a good deal of influence.

He decided to make Cripps Leader of the House: he felt that he would be a good advocate and that his brain would therefore be used in a manner suitable to it. . . .

All this was received by the Tory Party, who were not moved until the story of David's sacking came out[19]. . . .

You may now ask: 'What is the rival position of the various leaders?' The set-up, as I see it, is that the old wolf Winston is now surrounded by some young cubs, who will bite at his flanks. Max [Beaverbrook] regards this form of Government as a committee and thinks it will do in Winston. On the other hand, the cubs will give confidence to the public and will make Winston, I think, a better war leader – at any rate, for the immediate period ahead.

R. A. Butler to Sir Samuel Hoare, 6 March 1942: Lord Butler papers, Trinity College Cambridge, G14, ff. 33–4.

3.10 Churchill, Cripps and India

W. P. Crozier of the *Manchester Guardian* found when interviewing one of the government's most persistent critics that

[19] Conservatives were incensed at the manner of David Margesson's dismissal from the War Office, especially as he and Churchill regularly drank 'late at night' and 'behaved as two Harrovians together' – *Chuter Ede Diary*, 26 February 1942, p. 59.

nagging doubts about Churchill's ability to survive further setbacks continued into the spring of 1942.

9.30 a.m. Leslie Hore-Belisha, at 16 Stafford Place

He was animated and pretty positive regarding the Government's position. Cripps had just gone off to India and he said that it was truly remarkable that immediately after a so-called reconstruction of the Government in which Cripp's appointment was the only thing that mattered, Cripps should have been sent away to India.[20] 'Thus', he said, 'the "vitalising" influence that was to do so much for the Government, and therefore of which the public expected so much, has been sent out of the country, although certainly through his own volition. Incidentally, the man who would have been the strongest critical force has been taken into the War Cabinet.'

I inquired about the position of Cripps relatively to the Government when he came back to this country. 'Oh', he said, 'he was offered the Ministry of Supply and he would not take it but wanted a seat in the War Cabinet, and now that he has got it I believe that he has become a Moderate.' He said this in a semi-jesting manner with much amusement. I said 'What did you want him to do?' He replied 'I wanted him to stop out of the Government and to take the lead of all those people who are discontented with the way in which things are going and are anxious to get the war won with more energy and efficiency. Because if things are not changed we are going the right way as fast as we can to lose the war'. . . .

He then went on to talk about the effects of recent reverses on Churchill's prestige and on the effect which success or failure in India might be expected to have on Cripps's political fortunes when he came back. He also speculated as to who might be a successor to Churchill as Premier, and he said he wished very much there had been some way of calling in Lloyd George. He was a statesman, a great statesman, and it was deplorable that it hadn't been found possible to make use of his immense talents in spite of his age and of difficulties; he sincerely wished that it might still be possible.

Taylor (ed.), *Off the Record*: interview dated 20 March 1942.

[20] Cripps volunteered for a mission aimed at breaking the constitutional deadlock in India, made urgent by Japanese advances in the Far East.

3.11 'Winterton's Nightmare'

In spite of government changes, critics of the coalition such as Winterton were still concerned that the burden of running the war was being carried too heavily by one man.

David Low, Winterton's Nightmare, *Evening Standard*, 29 May 1942.

3.12 Disaster in North Africa

A fresh crisis for the government arose when it was suddenly announced that British forces had been defeated at Tobruk. As the Labour MP for the Forest of Dean later recounted, this led several backbenchers to question the whole handling of the war effort since 1940.

Perhaps the most useful thing that I was able to do in this Parliament . . . was to serve on the Select Committee for National Expenditure, although I had less experience of this kind of work than I had of agriculture and forestry.

In the first half of 1942 Japan swept all before her in the Pacific and the Far East. . . . As if this was not enough, in the summer of 1942 we met with near disaster in North Africa. Our tanks were not of the necessary calibre to stand up to the German tank in open fight. For two years past it was supposed that we had been designing and producing tanks, but when it came to the point at the second battle of Tobruk they failed in efficiency and fire power. So we lost Tobruk and twenty thousand of some of the best men in the Eighth Army. It turned out that some of our best designers had in 1940 been taken to work on aircraft, since after the fall of France and the imminence of invasion they were the most needed in the Battle of Britain. . . .

Our Select Committee now took it upon itself to enquire into all these facts. I was not on the Sub-Committee doing this, but at the full Committee saw the facts and they were horrifying. I looked at the documents, for the Committee had the power to order the War Office to let us see them. We saw them and gave them back at once: I would not have had them on my person for five seconds. I did not even dare to make a copy of some of the figures. They showed the whole position in North Africa as far as the tanks of both ourselves and the Axis Powers were concerned. At the full Committee then we discussed what we should do. Our duty was to report to the House in open session, but this we obviously could not do. We decided to report to the Speaker why we could not. . . .

Our Chairman, Sir John Wardlaw-Milne, then put a motion down for discussion in the House declaring our 'Lack of confidence in the central direction of the War'. It was supported by most of the members of the Committee and I too signed the motion. It was a strong thing to do, but I felt that it was justified because it turned out that there was not that co-operation between the various groups of scientific experts and the officials in the Admiralty and the War Office that was needed to produce the results. One group did not know what the other was doing. . . . We demanded that a scientific general staff should be created independent of the Departments concerned and with the right of direct access to the Prime Minister and the Cabinet. The Prime Minister, when we replied, was at first rather truculent, but then realised that we were not only in earnest but that we knew the facts. He became conciliatory and promised that he would look into the question of appointing a scientific general staff. At the time I thought that it would be better to accept this and not force the motion to a division; but our chairman would not withdraw the motion and it was heavily defeated. I myself abstained because at that moment it seemed as if Rommel might break through to Alexandria.

Morgan Philips Price, *My Three Revolutions*, London, 1969, pp. 278–9.

3.13 The Tobruk debate: Bevan's challenge

When the House of Commons came to discuss the Tobruk disaster, the Labour backbencher Aneurin Bevan, MP for Ebbw Vale, made a full-frontal assault that established his reputation as 'snarler in chief' against the government.

The Prime Minister wins Debate after Debate and loses battle after battle. . . .

It seems to me that there are three things wrong. First, the main strategy of the war has been wrong; second, the wrong weapons have been produced; and third, those weapons are being managed by men who are not trained in the use of them and who have not studied the use of modern weapons. As I understand it, it is strategy that dictates the weapon and tactics that dictate the use of the weapon. The Government has conceived the war wrongly from the very beginning, and no one has more misconceived it than the Prime Minister himself. The nature of the weapons used by the enemy has not been understood by the Prime Minister ever since the beginning of the war. . . .

If the Government think that there is any dismay in the country, they are wrong; there is anger in the country. This is a proud and brave race, and it is feeling humiliated. It cannot stand the holding out of Sebastopol for months and the collapse of Tobruk in 26 hours. It cannot stand the comparison between these lost battles, not lost by lack of courage, but by lack of vision at the top. It cannot stand this; it is a proud and valiant country, and it wants leadership. It is getting words, not leadership at the moment from the Government. There is only one way: Fight the enemy, for Heaven's sake fight him, wherever you can get at him. . . .

This nation can win; but it must be properly led, it must be properly inspired, and it must have confidence in its military leadership. Give us that, and we can win the war, in a fashion which will surprise Hitler, and at the same time hearten our friends.

Hansard, *Parliamentary Debates*, fifth series, vol. 381, 2 July 1942, cc. 528–40.

3.14 Outcome of the Tobruk debate

More dissatisfaction with Churchill's leadership was expressed in the Tobruk debate than at any time since May 1940, though the Prime Minister's position was made secure by an appalling gaffe from the main mover of the 'no confidence' motion.

1 July John Wardlaw-Milne moved his much publicised Vote of Censure in strong and convincing language today, and I watched the front bench squirm with annoyance. Winston looked harrassed and everyone was emotional and uneasy. I thought it all rather horrible. Wardlaw-Milne held the House well, he was fair, calm and dignified, and he was listened to with respect, until he made an unfortunate suggestion, that the Duke of Gloucester[21] should be made Commander-in-Chief of the forces. The House roared with disrespectful laughter, and I at once saw Winston's face light up, as if a lamp had been lit within and he smiled genially. He knew now that he was saved, and poor Wardlaw-Milne never quite regained the hearing of the House.

In the p.m. Oliver Lyttelton spoke for the Government and he made, as he afterwards remarked to Somerset de Chair, 'a proper balls of it'. His canvas was too large, he was too diffuse and altogether too unconvincing. He suffered a parliamentary setback, and I did not wait to hear him finish, thus missed Clem Davies' novel suggestion that he should be impeached. . . .

2 July Today Belisha made what proved to be a brilliant, eloquent and damning attack on the Government. He was skilful and deadly, and I admired his courage and accurate marshalling of the

[21] Brother of King George VI.

facts. Surely Churchill, I thought, could not answer him, but answer him he did, and for over an hour we had all the usual Churchillian gusto. . . . But his magic had no magic for me, we might as well have Macaulay or even Caruso as Prime Minister. He skated around dangerous corners, and by clever evasion managed to ignore the question as to whether he had ordered Tobruk to be held. Nevertheless he had his usual effect of intoxicating his listeners. I left before he sat down and went to the library, put my head into my hands, took a deep breath and prayed for advice. . . . The argument against voting against the Government is strong and, on balance, I decided I hadn't 'the guts', so slowly walked into the very crowded Aye Lobby to the derision of the few abstainers, perhaps 20 in all. I saw Winterton and Archie Southby muttering to one another. They had abstained, as had Lady Astor, Megan Lloyd George and others who sat silent on the benches.[22] I waited until the final figures were announced. 475 to 25, a Government majority of 450. The PM rose, looked up at the Speaker's Gallery, smiled at Mrs Churchill, and then walked out of the Chamber to go to the Smoking Room. As he left he received a polite but lukewarm ovation.

Rhodes James (ed.), *Channon Diary*, 1–2 July 1942, pp. 334–5.

3.15 A breathing space for the Prime Minister

Some backbenchers were convinced that victory in the Tobruk debate only gave Churchill a breathing space, and that further military defeats would ensure his downfall. In the meantime, speculation continued about possible successors.

If Alexandria had fallen, Winston would have fallen also. As it is, he will hold his position until we get another major reverse. . . . As far as sheer competence in waging war is concerned, there is no one in the country who can hold a candle to Winston, and, if we open a second front in the near future, I cannot think of anyone better fitted to direct it. My complaint against him is not the one commonly made, that he overrules his service chiefs. . . . We have not, in fact, had any of the typically Churchillian strokes in this war. I wish he would use

[22] Nancy Astor, Tory MP for Plymouth Sutton; Megan Lloyd George, Liberal MP for Anglesey.

more forcefully his martial experience. . . . In a democratic country, however, a Prime Minister needs more than merit: he must also command general approval. It must be confessed that Winston's stock has been falling badly. This ought to be a 'People's War', but Winston has never, owing to his background and record, been able to capture the affections of the working classes as L.G. did. . . . [As a result] there will be a change in time, and inevitably (though possibly after a short interlude) Cripps will be PM. . . . Whatever the Gallup Poll may reveal . . . a large number in both the Labour Party and the Conservative Party regard Eden as a weak figure who has got his present position only by birth, the right school, good looks and luck. The Conservatives, anxious to avoid Eden, are at present canvassing R. A. Butler as PM! . . . The bulk of the Labour Party would prefer Cripps to Attlee, and combined with the Tory feeling I have mentioned, this will bring Cripps to the top. I repeat this conviction even though Cripps' stock in Left circles has fallen heavily, both in the House and outside, since he joined the Cabinet.

Ivor Thomas[23] to Tom Jones, 13 August 1942: Lord Astor papers, Reading University Library, MS1066/823, cited in P. Addison, *The Road to 1945*, London, 1975, pp. 208–9.

3.16 **Cripps determines to resign**

> Stafford Cripps had certainly not given up ambitions of replacing the Prime Minister. During the autumn of 1942 he was making clear his determination to resign, thereby giving himself the freedom to criticise from the back-benches; his grounds for doing so were outlined in this letter to Churchill.

In my view the present method of conducting affairs is unsatisfactory and is too much on a 'hand-to-mouth' basis. When I first joined the Government you will recollect that I pointed out that in my view it was necessary to have a War Cabinet of non-departmental Ministers which could act as central 'thinking and planning machine' in connection with the whole conduct of the war strategically, domestically and internationally. As I had been out of the country for nearly two

[23] Labour MP for Keighley.

years and had had no experience of the actual machine of government as it had developed during the war, I did not then make any other precise suggestions. Since then I have done my best to familiarise myself with the organisation and administration of government and I am more than ever convinced of the necessity of such a War Cabinet.

At the present time there does not exist any body, either political or technical, which can or does give concentrated and continual thought to all these matters. The practical effect is that problems of strategy are conceived by the War Cabinet hurriedly, without sufficient information and often in isolation. . . . A War Cabinet which sometimes meets only once a week and then with ten to fifteen other people present cannot really be said to be 'conducting' the war, especially when three of its seven members are not on the Defence Committee and have no knowledge of the discussions and decisions in that committee. Under such conditions it is not right, in my view, that the War Cabinet should appear to carry responsibility for the conduct of the war, since it is not in a position to discharge that responsiblity. . . .

There is another major matter which I mentioned in my last note and which I have many times brought up in different forms since the very beginning of the war. That is the need to give the people some more definite prospect for the future. This is closely linked with the necessity for an alteration in the present attitude towards the finances of the war effort. I regard both these matters as having a direct and immediate bearing on our hopes for victory. So far the 'inducement' offered to greater effort has largely been financial in the form of increased wages, increased pay, larger profits, etc. For this should be substituted the inducement of service and sacrifice in the national cause. The reward should be what we are fighting for and not what people can get now. To the younger people especially, the question of the future is of very great importance.

I fully appreciate and understand the view you have taken of these matters. As you have stated, if you are to run the war, you must run it your own way. As to the future, you believe that all energy must be concentrated on the immediate task in hand and you do not regard post-war arrangements as any part of that task, besides which, their discussion is apt to raise political differences, which is undesirable. Nevertheless, I feel compelled to express to you these very definite views which I hold, as I believe their adoption to be, broadly speaking, essential for the success of our war effort.

Stafford Cripps to Winston Churchill, 21 September 1942, reprinted in C. Cooke, *The Life of Richard Stafford Cripps*, London, 1957, pp. 298–9.

3.17 The battle in North Africa

Writing after the war with the benefit of notes made in 1942, the Prime Minister's doctor recalled how the combination of a major battle in North Africa and Cripps' threat to resign caused great anxiety in Downing Street.

In 1953 I asked Winston to pick out the two most anxious months of the war. He did not hesitate: 'September and October, yes, 1942'. And yet, if I can trust my diary, I was not unduly worried about him then. It is true that whenever I appeared at No. 10, there seemed to be some fresh burden on his mind, but he met these calls with such abounding energy that I felt his reserves had hardly been touched. . . .

The Prime Minister was still living on his balance at the bank that had accumulated in 1940. Broadly speaking, he got his way in everything. . . . But the P.M. knew how far he could go. He knew that the resignation of the Leader of the House on such as issue as the conduct of the war must lead to a political crisis of the first magnitude. During September, the P.M. used all his powers of persuasion to convert Cripps, and in the end Cripps, whose high sense of duty had never been in question, was persuaded to postpone his resignation until after the battle in the desert. . . .

September 30, 1942

Brendan Bracken came to see me today. He says that if Rommel is victorious the position of the Prime Minister will become very difficult. 'You see, Charles, important changes in the direction of the war would then be inevitable, and Winston will never submit to any curtailment of his powers. If we are beaten in this battle, it's the end of Winston. Is he sleeping alright? You see, he is going though a very bad time'. . . .

I can see now that I was completely taken in by the bold front the P.M. put up during those two critical months. . . . He knew what defeat would mean. Brendan did not exaggerate the turmoil in his mind when he said: 'Winston is finding the suspense almost unbearable.' Greedily he devoured the reports from the desert. It appeared that everyone in the Eighth Army was cock-a-hoop when the battle began on October 23.

The Prime Minister and his colleagues in the Cabinet were therefore both surprised and shocked when, after a week's hard slogging, there was nothing to show for 10,000 casualties. The offensive seemed little nearer its goal than at the beginning. When I had to see the P.M. about a sleeping pill, they warned me that he was in an explosive mood. I was with him only a few moments, but as I left he grunted half under his breath: 'If this goes on, anything may happen.' I found Brooke[24] waiting for me. 'Is the P.M. all right, Charles? I thought he was going to hit me when he demanded: "Haven't we got a single general who can even win one battle?"'

Lord Moran, *Winston Churchill: The Struggle for Survival 1940–1965*, London, 1966, pp. 90 and 95–6.

3.18 **Victory at El Alamein**

When news came through that British troops had finally secured a major victory at El Alamein, criticism of Churchill's leadership at last evaporated, and the threat from Cripps was suddenly nullified.

It was this morning, going round Pattisons Mills at Whitehaven, that a police inspector first told us the news of the American landings in French North Africa. And so, through this amazing weekend and the next days, the news poured in. 'This is not the end; it is not even the beginning of the end, but it is perhaps the end of the beginning.' In this admirable and characteristic phrase, the P.M. two days later summed up the situation. I said, 'We can see the great tide turning today on the North African beaches.' This, following so fast on the great victory of the Eighth Army, changes both the immediate, and the ultimate, prospects of the war, and still more changes all our feelings. The critics of the 'higher direction of the war' – the Shinwells and the Belishas and the rest – will all have sunk well out of

[24] Field Marshal Sir Alan Brooke, Chief of the Imperial General Staff.

sight and mind today. And Crazy Cripps will have to think again about the prospect of the P.M. falling from power and find some new excuse for his own resignation from the Government, in time, as he sees it, to save part of . . .his 'mystique'.[25]

Pimlott (ed.), *Second World War Diary of Hugh Dalton*: entry for 8 November 1942, pp. 514–15.

3.19 **Reflecting on the crisis of 1942**

The Labour minister Chuter Ede noted that although Churchill survived the traumas of 1942, it had been a close run thing. His reflections on the past year also pointed to the issue that was to dominate British politics for the remainder of the war – reconstruction.

This is the end of one of the great years in the history of mankind. It has seen great changes in the mood of Englishmen. Its early months became successively more & more depressing with the spread of Japanese domination over the possessions of Britain, the Netherlands & the U.S.A. in the Far East & the Pacific. Then came the defeats of the British in North Africa. I do not think even the collapse of France made me as miserable as did the fall of Tobruk. The faith of everyone was sorely tried & though the Vote of Confidence only had 25 supporters in the lobby misgivings were profound. The Communists' constant demand for a Second Front in Europe & their insinuations that we were failing our Allies added to the feeling of frustration. Then followed months of stagnation, disturbed only by the raid on Dieppe. This apparent inaction still further tried our faith. Had anyone seen an alternative to Churchill the Government would have fallen. Then on 21st October came the speech by Smuts[26] to both Houses in which he said we were passing to the offensive stage of the war. I noted on 25th October . . .'In the 1 o'clock news today it was announced that the 8th Army had started an offensive in Egypt.' After so many previous disillusionments one received the news of the next few days with every caution. On 4th

[25] In the event, Churchill carried out a small ministerial reshuffle, removing Cripps from the War Cabinet and sending him to the Ministry of Aircraft Production.
[26] Field Marshal Jan Smuts, veteran South African leader.

Nov. the P[resident of the Board of Education] told me the P.M. thought the battle was going well. On 5th Nov. the P. gave me the first hint that a U.S.A. landing in Africa was expected. Then the news became outspokenly cheerful. A great revulsion of feeling occured & the P.M.'s patient & skilful planning became manifest. Even the Darlan incident[27] failed to shake the confidence newly reposed spontaneously in him by the House, especially after hearing him in Secret Session. The tremendous hammer blows since struck by the Russians have confirmed the view that the Allies have in Europe & Africa the initiative. The road ahead may yet be long but in these theatres we can glimpse the summit of the pass. . . . We have shown no signs of being able to attack the homelands of Japan. The position of the Chinese, after 5½ years of war, causes anxiety. Yet, taking all in all, our cause looks better in prospect tonight than we could have expected twelve months ago. Our situation, though still grave, has vastly improved since October. . . .

I think the Tories mean to dish the Labour Party of any great measure of social improvement, but Ernest Bevin is a tougher Labour statesman than any they have encountered.

Jefferys (ed.), *Chuter Ede Diary*, 31 December 1942, pp. 115-16.

[27] This stemmed from the willingness of the American commander, Eisenhower, to enlist the support in North Africa of Admiral Darlan, a notorious Nazi collaborator.

4
The Beveridge Report and reconstruction

For more than two years after Churchill came to power in May 1940, the government's energies were focused on matters of military strategy and production. This did not, however, prevent a burgeoning debate about Britain's domestic future and the possibility of creating a 'New Jerusalem'. Publication of the immensely popular Beveridge Report late in 1942 brought social reform to the centre of the political stage, and the subsequent appointment of Minister of Reconstruction represented a serious attempt to co-ordinate proposals for change. The second half of the war thus witnessed a more active phase of reconstruction policy, with the government outlining its commitment to reform in a series of white papers. But, as the extracts in this chapter indicate, the extent to which Churchill moved towards a 'welfare state' remains questionable. Ministers ultimately promised more than they delivered, hamstrung by the knowledge that deep-seated differences continued to exist between Conservative and Labour wings of the coalition.

4.1 A brave new world?

The threat of imminent invasion in 1940 generated the feeling that a brave new world would have to be created if Britain survived the war; such sentiment was reflected even in newspapers not hitherto noted for their commitment to social change.

The anniversary of the signing of the Versailles Treaty[1] passed at the week-end unhonoured and almost unnoticed. Twenty years of disillusionment and crisis have quenched the facile idealism and no less facile optimism which marked the end of the last War, and have encouraged the cynic to see in the present war nothing more than a clash of rival imperialisms struggling for the mastery. This view is not, however, shared by the great masses of people in this country or by their friends abroad. Inexorable events have thrust into the background the discussions about war aims which were so popular in the first months of the war. That is necessary and right. The Prime Minister expressed the mood of the nation when he declared that our only present war aim is victory. Nevertheless the British will to victory is still bound up with the conviction that our war aims stand on a different plane from those of the enemy, and that victory for our arms will point the way to a new social and international order in Europe. . . .

Over the greater part of Western Europe the common values for which we stand are known and prized. We must indeed beware of defining these values in purely nineteenth-century terms. If we speak of democracy we do not mean a democracy which maintains the right to vote but forgets the right to work and the right to live. If we speak of freedom we do not mean a rugged individualism which excludes social organisation and economic planning. If we speak of equality we do not mean a political equality nullified by social and economic privilege. If we speak of economic reconstruction we think less of maximum (though this job too will be required) than of equitable distribution. The attacks of the dictators on 'Pluto democracy' are an effort partly to exploit the impoverishment they have created and partly to conceal its cause. The plea is grotesque enough especially in the conclusions which the dictators seek to draw from it. But the persistence of these attacks and the purpose which they are intended to serve abroad may remind us that the problem of the new order is social as well as international. The European house cannot be put in order unless we put our own house in order first. The new order cannot be based on the preservation of privilege whether the privilege be that of a country, of a class or of an individual.

The Times, 1 July 1940.

[1] The peace treaty which imposed harsh terms upon Germany at the end of the First World War.

4.2 Britain's war aims

The Prime Minister effectively blocked any far-reaching discussion of war aims by his government colleagues. His insistence that the war came first, relayed in this extract by his secretary, helps to explain why planning for the domestic future received such a low priority in the dark days of 1940–41.

In a telegram to the Prime Ministers of Australia and New Zealand, promising that we will abandon the Mediterranean and send our fleet eastwards in the event of Japan attacking Australia or N.Z., Winston has written: 'If Hitler fails to invade and conquer Britain before the weather breaks, he has received his first and probably fatal check'. . . .

Later on, at lunch, Winston gave me his own views about war aims and the future. He said there was only one war aim, to destroy Hitler. Let those who say they do not know what they are fighting for stop fighting and they will see. After the last war people had done much constructive thinking and the League of Nations had been a magnificent idea. Something of the kind would have to be built up again: there would a United States of Europe, and this Island would be the link connecting this Federation with the new world and able to hold the balance between the two. . . .

I lunched en famille with the P.M., Mrs C. and Mary,[2] and it could not have been more enjoyable. Winston was in the best of humours. He talked brilliantly on every topic from Ruskin to Lord Baldwin, from the future of Europe to the strength of the Tory Party. . . . He said that the Tory Party was the strength of the country: few things needed to be changed quickly and drastically; what conservatism, as envisaged by Disraeli, stood for was the gradual increase of amenities for an ever larger number of the people, who should enjoy the benefits previously reserved for a very few (i.e. a levelling upwards, not a levelling downwards). . . .

Colville, *Fringes of Power*: entry for 10 August 1940, pp. 215–6.

[2] Churchill's wife, Clemmie, and his daughter, later Mary Soames.

4.3 The Prime Minister and education policy

The manner of Rab Butler's appointment as education minister in 1941 was a further indication that Churchill was in no mood to push post-war questions up the political agenda.

I went on serving at the Foreign Office under Anthony Eden . . . until, in the summer of 1941, I was given my opportunity to harness to the educational system the wartime urge for social reform and greater equality. . . .

In the spring 'Gil' Winant, the American Ambassador, came down to stay with us, feeling very strained, but as usual full of confidence in our future. . . . He forecast to me that England would go Socialist after the war: I knew no one else whose instinct made them so sure. He also said that I ought to take over the Board of Education 'when the present man goes'. I asked him whether he had got this idea from Brendan Bracken; but he said, 'No. I thought it out for myself. This is where you can influence the future of England.'

I was strongly drawn to Winant's idea, while still doubting whether it had been entirely self-generated. And it was not long afterwards that the ubiquitous Brendan Bracken informed me that the Prime Minister's friends desired to 'make a complete break with the past and the Munich period', and that he thought [education minister] Herwald Ramsbotham would shortly retire, leaving a vacancy for me at Education. . . .

Ten days later, the Prime Minister sent for me. He saw me after his afternoon nap and was purring like a tiger. He began, 'You have been in the House fifteen years and it is time you were promoted.' I objected gently that I had been there only twelve years but he waved this aside. 'You have been in the government for the best part of that time and I now want you to go to the Board of Education. I think that you can leave your mark there. You will be independent. Besides', he continued, with rising fervour, 'you will be in the war. You will move poor children from here to here', and he lifted up and evacuated imaginery children from one side of his blotting pad to the other; 'this will be very difficult'. . . . I then said that I had always looked forward to going to the Board of Education if I were given the chance. He appeared ever so slightly surprised at this, showing that he felt that in wartime a central job, such as the one I was leaving, is the most important.

Butler, *Art of the Possible*, pp. 86–90.

4.4 The '1918 trick'

Many Labour MPs saw domestic reform as their price of participation in the coalition. The frustration caused by lack of real progress on reconstruction was noted by the party's junior education minister, talking here to his political chief about the prospect of educational reform.

Friday 7 August I went up . . . and reached the Board [of Education] just before 10.30. . . . I stood out strongly for a Bill next session. The Labour Party wanted something on account & we were most easily able to provide it. The P[resident of the Board, R. A. Butler] said he was submitting a paper making benefits through the education service an alternative to the Beveridge Report which would cost 650 millions a year. The education benefits could be obtained for 100 millions a year.

Friday 27 November The P. said he thought we were moving steadily. Had I heard if Greenwood had yet met the Cardinal?[3] I said I did not know, but I expected he was too busy with next week's debate on Reconstruction. I added that the Labour Party were getting suspicious that the 1918 trick would be worked on them again; they sensed a feeling among the Tories that we should be kept in the Govt. until victory was assured & that then we should be pushed out & the world made safe for 1939 standards. There would therefore be a growing demand for something on account. The Liberals would feel the same. The P. said that suited him down to the ground for the young Tories felt that way too. . . . The P.M. was watching us with some amusement thinking we were squelching about in the mud & were not going to get anything. If we did make real progress, the P.M. would want the thing done – he was like that.

Jefferys (ed.), *Chuter Ede Diary*: entries for 7 August and 27 November 1942, pp. 92 and 109–10.

4.5 The Beveridge Report

The many scattered discussions about the future of Britain were

[3] Greenwood was due to discuss educational reform with Cardinal Hinsley, Roman Catholic Archbishop of Westminster.

suddenly given focus by the publication late in 1942 of the Beveridge Report,[4] a detailed study of the principles and practice of social insurance.

300. *Scope of Social Security:* The term 'social security' is used here to denote the securing of an income to take the place of earnings when they are interrupted by unemployment, sickness or accident, to provide for the retirement through age, to provide against loss of support by the death of another person, and to meet exceptional expenditures, such as those connected with birth, death and marriage. Primarily social security means security of income up to a minimum, but the provision of an income should be associated with treatment designed to bring the interruption of earning to an end as soon as possible.

301. *Three Assumptions:* No satisfactory scheme of social security can be devised except on the following assumptions:

(a) Children's allowances for children up to the age of 15 or if in full-time education up to the age of 16;

(b) Comprehensive health and re-habilitation of services for prevention and cure of disease and restoration of capacity for work, available to all members of the community;

(c) Maintenance of employment, that is to say avoidance of mass unemployment. . . .

302. *Three Methods of Security:* On these three assumptions, a Plan for Social Security is outlined below, combining three distinct methods: social insurance for basic needs; national assistance for special cases; voluntary insurance for additions to the basic provision. . . .

304. *Flat Rate of Subsistence Benefit:* The first fundamental principle of the social insurance scheme is provision of a flat rate of insurance benefit, irrespective of the amount of the earnings which have been interrupted by unemployment or disability or ended by retirement. . . .

305. *Flat Rate of Contribution:* The second fundamental principle of the scheme is that the compulsory contribution required of each insured person or his employer is a flat rate, irrespective of his means. All insured persons, rich or poor, will pay the same contributions for the same security; those with larger means will pay more

[4] Sir William Beveridge was a distinguished civil servant and former Director of the London School of Economics.

only to the extent that as tax-payers they pay more to the National Exchequer and so the State share of the Social Insurance Fund. . . .

306. *Unification of Administrative Responsibility:* The third fundamental principle is unification of administrative responsibility in the interests of efficiency and economy. For each insured person there will be a single weekly contribution, in respect of all his benefits. . . . All contributions will be paid into a single Social Insurance Fund and all benefits and other insurance payments will be paid from that fund.

307. *Adequacy of Benefit:* The fourth fundamental principle is adequacy of benefit in amount and in time. The flat rate of benefit proposed is intended to be sufficient without further resources to provide the minimum income needed for subsistence in all normal cases. . . .

308. *Comprehensiveness:* The fifth fundamental principle is that social insurance should be comprehensive, in respect of the persons covered and of their needs. . . .

309. *Classification:* The sixth fundamental principle is that social insurance, while unified and comprehensive, must take account of the different ways of life of different sections of the community; of those dependent on earnings by employment under contract of service, of those earning in other ways, of those rendering vital unpaid service as housewives, of those not yet of age to earn and of those past earning.

Report on Social Insurance and Alliance Services, Cmd. 6404, London, 1942, pp. 120–2.

4.6 Public reaction to the Report

The Report received a remarkable public reception, aided by wide publicity and a series of explanatory pamphlets, which sold out almost overnight. Mass-Observation recorded numerous responses, indicating the sex (M or F), age and social class (from A at top of economic scale to D at bottom) of each respondant.

M45D (2.12.42)

. . . it will make the ordinary man think that the country at last has some regard for him as he is supposed to have regard for the country.

M50D (2.12.42)

If it has taken a War to make a Government see how urgent is the need for improving conditions of the smaller fry, then we have not fought the war for nothing.

F45B (2.12.42)

Had read the summary of the proposals.
A most worthy attempt to improve the lot of the people at large but hoped it would not lead to a large number of workers being satisfied with being unemployed, owing to increase in the benefit rate.

M45C (2.12.42)

Read the table of proposals and thought they were just what was needed. It should certainly be passed & I would not give much for the future chance of any Party that opposed it.

F30B (3.12.42)

It's a wonderful plan, of course, but I don't know if it will come to anything. There's such a lot will stand out against it. Big business and all that.

F23C (3.12.42)

I haven't read all the details. I gather he's making us happy for ever after.

M35B (3.12.42)

It's extraordinary the interest people are taking in it. When I went down to the Stationery Office to get it there were queues of people buying it, & I was looking at it on the bus & the conductor said 'I suppose you haven't got a spare copy of that?'

F35B (3.12.42)

. . . I'm not an idealist. I'm selfish. I only think of myself. I know all is changing but I resent it. I've been one of the lucky few and I want to remain so. I had a good life. I know there's poverty of the many on one side and great luxury of the few. But I hate to see the great houses go, the fine estates and the gracious living. . . .

I think we pamper the workers, especially in the factories, with their canteens and music. They ought to work harder.

F40C (5.12.42)

It's good isn't it. Yes. Something to look forward to. We might not all be so poor then. But it's not passed yet, is it. It's got to go through Parliament.

P. Thomas (ed.), *Mass-Observation in World War II. Post-War Hopes & Expectations and Reaction to the Beveridge Report*, University of Sussex Library, 1988.

4.7 Left-wing reaction to the Beveridge plan

The Report was acclaimed by Labour as the type of reform advocated by the left for many years. This enthusiasm was shared even by critics, such as Nye Bevan and *Tribune*, who had taken the lead in attacking Labour ministers for not pressing hard enough to introduce reconstruction measures.

In a general sense the decision to allow a report on social conditions to appear at this time was the work of a guilty national conscience. No return to the conditions of the past were thought possible. The Left were demanding the pledge of a new world. The Right . . . realised the perils of withstanding concession. No doubt they believed that a goodly array of burnished platitudes would stay the avalanche of public opinion until they were stronger for the fight and until their conscience had relapsed into its old accustomed inertia. Nothing else can explain the political lunacy (from their point of view) of Mr Churchill and his friends which has tolerated the publication of Sir William's findings. For the mouse has been in labour and has brought forth a mountain.

Sir William Beveridge is a social evangelist of the old Liberal school. He is an honoured member of the Reform Club, and the horizon of his political aspirations is, therefore, not boundless. He specifically disavows many of the tenets of revolutionary Socialism. But he has a good heart and a clear, well-stocked head, and he has discharged his task with Liberal fervour and even a trace of Liberal innocence.

What kind of world would the honest Liberal like to establish? He would like to make a truce between private enterprise and State ownership. He would like the two to work in harness together, but, above all, he would like, by resolute action, to appease the most obvious pains and to succour the most grievous casualties which capitalism produces. From this dangerous angle Sir William has approached his task. He would like to establish a tolerable minimum standard of security for every citizen, for the injured worker, for the widow, for the aged, for the unemployed, for the sick and for the growing child.

This is a commendable ambition, and the desire to achieve it is certainly not confined to those who have dabbled or delved into Socialism. But the merit and novelty of Sir William is that he has set down with the authority of a statistician and on Government notepaper the conditions which must be satisfied if this modest ambition is to be achieved. Here it is in black and white – a plain description of man's necessities, how much (or how little) he must have in his pocket if fear and want and hunger are to be lifted from his cares and if the grandiloquent phrases of the Atlantic Charter[5] are to be translated into fact. In short, Sir William has described the conditions in which the tears might be taken out of capitalism.

Tribune, 4 December 1942.

4.8 The Prime Minister's response

Enthusiasm for the Beveridge scheme was not shared by the Prime Minister, as he made clear in this memorandum to his cabinet colleagues.

1. A dangerous optimism is growing up about the conditions it will be possible to establish here after the war. Unemployment and low wages are to be abolished, education greatly improved and prolonged; great developments in housing and health will be undertaken; agriculture is to be maintained at least at its new high level. At the same time the cost of living is not to be raised. The Beveridge plan of social insurance, or something like it, is to abolish want. . . .

2. Our foreign investments have almost disappeared. The United States will be a strong competitor with British shipping. We shall have great difficulties in placing our necessary exports profitably.

[5] The 1941 agreement between Britain and the United States which declared the right of all nations to democratic elections and protection from foreign domination.

Meanwhile, in order to help Europe, we are to subject ourselves to a prolonged period of rationing and distribute a large part of our existing stocks. . . . We must clearly keep a large Air Force and Navy, so as not to be set upon again by the Germans, and large military forces will be needed to garrison the enemy countries and make sure they do not begin to rearm for revenge.

3. The question steals across the mind whether we are not committing our forty-five million people to task beyond their compass, and laying on them burdens beyond their capacity to bear. While not disheartening our people by dwelling on the dark side of things, Ministers should, in my view, be careful not to raise false hopes, as was done last time by speeches about 'homes for heroes', etc. The broad masses of the people face the hardships of life undaunted, but they are liable to get very angry if they feel they have been gulled or cheated. . . . It is because I do not wish to deceive the people by false hopes and airy visions of Utopia and Eldorado that I have refrained so far from making promises about the future.

4. We must all do our best, and we shall do it much better if we are not hampered by a cloud of pledges and promises which arise out of the hopeful and genial side of man's nature and are not brought into relation with the hard facts of life.

'Promises about Post-War Conditions', Note circulated to the cabinet by the Prime Minister, 12 January 1943, reprinted in Winston S. Churchill, *The Second World War*, Vol. IV, *The Hinge of Fate*, London, 1951, pp. 861–2.

4.9 The Beveridge debate in the House of Commons

As a compromise between left and right, the cabinet agreed to welcome the Beveridge Report in principle but without making any commitment to early introduction. Ministerial attempts to justify this approach, however, led to consternation on the Labour benches in the House of Commons.

Tuesday 16 February Sir John Anderson . . . read every word from a carefully prepared typescript.[6] His speech was completely

[6] Anderson was responsible for stating government policy in his capacity as Lord President of the Council.

humourless. He devoted a long time to the difficulties of our present situation. He made everyone think, as he spoke to a running and approving murmur of Tory die-hard cheers, that the Govt. would shelve the whole matter. Aneurin Bevan tried to get his reading stopped by the Speaker, declaring that there was obviously no Govt. pronouncment being made. He had little sympathy from the House except Stokes;[7] he satirically suggested the speech should be circulated. After a time Anderson dealt with the Beveridge proposals seriatim. He gave specific pledges but the House had been so deadened by the preliminary lugubrious remarks that they just could not grasp that something was to be done. He did not make the value of child welfare schemes clear and Evelyn Walkden[8] intervened to point [out] that the present meals were paid for by the parents. In setting out arguments for & against certain courses Anderson always seemed to speak with more conviction against Beveridge than for him, although generally he came down on Beveridge's side. The Labour Party appeared to support him in deciding to make the scheme universal & to alter the separate bases of approved societies, but they were vocally hostile to the continuation of voluntary hospitals. On the whole I think they were greatly disappointed. This I am sure is more due to the presentation than to the decisions of the Govt. . . .

Wednesday 17 February The papers this morning indicate that an acute political crisis has arisen over Anderson's speech. The Administrative Committee of the Labour Party have put down an amendment to Greenwood's motion on the Beveridge Report.

Jefferys (ed.), *Chuter Ede diary*: entries for 16–17 February 1943, pp. 119–20.

4.10 Labour's amendment to the Beveridge motion

In response to the speech by Sir John Anderson, Labour MPs decided to press for the immediate implementation of the Beveridge Report. The mover of Labour's amendment, James Griffiths, later reflected on the debate and its long-term electoral effects.

[7] Richard Stokes, Labour MP for Ipswich.
[8] Labour MP for Doncaster.

When arrangements were made for a three-day debate on the Beveridge Plan in February 1943 it was at first agreed that it should take place on a motion supported by all parties in the coalition, as it was made known that Churchill was anxious there should be no division on Beveridge. He had appointed a Cabinet committee to consider the proposals and deputed the chairman, Sir John Anderson, to open the debate from the Government benches. It turned out to be one of Churchill's errors of judgement. John Anderson (later Lord Waverley) had enjoyed an immense reputation as one of the ablest of top civil servants. . . . He was known as a man who counted every penny twice and so was the worst possible choice as chairman of the Government's committee on post-war reconstruction. His speech in the debate was so full of 'ifs' and 'buts' that it caused obvious embarrassment to his colleagues on the Government benches, and infuriated ours. To add to our misgivings another civil servant turned minister, Sir James Grigg,[9] refused to allow a summary of the Beveridge Plan to be circulated to the forces on the grounds that to do so would have 'conveyed the impression that the scheme was settled Government policy, whereas in fact no decision of any kind had been taken'. The speech by Anderson, and the veto by Grigg, confirmed our fears that the reactionaries within the Government had carried the day. At a meeting of the party during the second day of the debate it was resolved, notwithstanding impassioned appeals by Ernest Bevin and Herbert Morrison, to table a motion expressing dissatisfaction with the Government's attitude to the Beveridge Plan, and to carry our motion to a division. I was entrusted with the task of moving our resolution and, though it was defeated by 325 votes to 119, the long-term effects of the division were important.

Sir William Beveridge has recorded how, at the end of the division, I said to him: 'This debate, and the division, makes the return of a Labour Government to power at the next election a certainty.'

James Griffiths, *Pages from Memory*, London, 1969, pp. 71–2.

[9] Secretary of State for War 1942–45.

4.11 The climax of the debate: the coalition divided

At the time of the debate Labour ministers were far from sure that benefits would result for the party. As Hugh Dalton noted, he and others in government were placed in the awkward position of being in the opposite division lobby to all Labour backbenchers, a situation which raised the possibility of the break-up of the coalition.

Third day of the Beveridge debate. Meeting of . . . Parliamentary Party at 10. . . . Bevin speaks at the Party Meeting and makes a mess of it. He begins quite well by pointing out that there are many things in Beveridge which are not acceptable to the trade unions, or on which consultation with the trade unions will be necessary. Therefore, they should not swallow Beveridge whole. So far so good, but he then begins to shout, protest and threaten, which he is always too much apt to do, and which undoes it all. He says the Party amendment is a vote of censure on him . . . and that, if this is the way things are to be done, he will refuse to go on. . . . Barnes[10] makes a good speech immediately afterwards and turns them all against Bevin, saying that if anyone threatens to resign because they are unwilling to accept the view of the majority, that resignation should be accepted. This is loudly cheered by an excited Meeting . . . [which] finally votes, practically unanimously, to divide on its own amendment. . . .

Morrison, winding up for the Government, makes a grand speech. I am quite sure that if this had been made on the first day, there would have been no crisis at all. But it is by now much too late to retrieve the ground lost by Anderson and Kingsley Wood, or to stop most of the Party voting for their amendment against the Government. . . . At least twenty-four of our members, who remain in the House till the end, don't vote. . . . The minority vote, 119, is nearly the same as that in the Tory revolt against the Catering Bill, 116.[11] Of the 119, 98 are Labour members, the rest being Liberals and other oddments. But no Tories.

I return a little weary to the Board of Trade. We cannot have many more such incidents. This one has been incredibly mishandled by all

[10] Alfred Barnes, Labour MP for East Ham South.

[11] Ernest Bevin's proposal to introduce Trade Boards into the catering profession was carried by 283 votes to 116. More Conservatives opposed the plan (111) than gave it support (107).

concerned from start to finish, except by Morrison. But what a lot of our Members don't see is that they run a risk of the P.M. appealing to the country, on the grounds that he must know where he stands, with the result that the Labour Party would be scrubbed out as completely as in 1931. As Wilmot and I agree, many of our colleagues are complete innocents, while a small minority is fixedly set on breaking up the Government. Master Shinwell today has been rushing about with a maniacal glint in his eye. He reminds me of the chap who was determined to set fire to the house and burn it down for his own delight.

Pimlott (ed.), *Second World War Diary of Hugh Dalton*: entry for 18 February 1943, pp. 554–6.

4.12 **Churchill's Four-Year Plan**

Following the parliamentary debate, Churchill decided upon further official investigation into the Beveridge proposals. In the meantime, the Prime Minister also formulated an ambitious Four-Year Plan, though his commitment to the scheme was questioned in private comments made to W. P. Crozier of the *Manchester Guardian*.

12.45 p.m. Winston Churchill

He was the usual mixture of grimness and good-humour. It was, he said, 'with great resentment' that he found himself being constantly told that he must talk about post-war plans when we had nothing like won the war. People were always getting ahead of events. He was dismayed when he opened his paper on the morning after the break-through on the Mareth coastal stretch. From the headlines 'you would have thought that we were in Tunis already, so, when I got the bad news of the setback, I went straight down to the House and gave everyone a stiff warning'.

Then he reverted to his broadcast. I said that traces of 'resentment' came out at the beginning and at the end, and he said 'Well, anyhow, I did it – and I took three weeks to think over what I was going to say.' Then he got on to the domestic politics of the broadcast. 'I don't know at all what Labour are going to do. I don't want them to come out of the Government and, on the whole, I don't think they will. I think they'll finally decide to go on – perhaps for another twelve months anyway. I don't want a General Election – not if it can be avoided. . . . But, however much I dislike it, I might have to do it – if they [opponents whoever they might be] created such a state of things that we could not get on efficiently with the war'. . . .

We then got on to the four-year plan and the question of how much should be put through Parliament before the election. I said I thought it would be a great mistake, and the country would be much disappointed, if it was understood that the election was to be followed not by the carrying into action of plans already passed but by long sessions of *legislative* debates. He said, 'Well, but I included in my speech legislative preparation. There will be all kinds of preparation – some administrative and some legislative. There's a lot of preparation going on now – as e.g. with regard to building. There's going to be legislation about education. There will be other things. But, regarding this insurance question, I don't think that the time and energies of Parliament ought to be distracted, because they *would* be distracted to the details of a great programme like that, instead of devoting its mind mainly to the job of the actual war. I feel that most strongly. And a great deal depends, of course, on the length of the war and how much time we have.'

Taylor (ed.), *Off the Record*: interview dated 26 March 1943, pp. 345–7.

4.13 **Pressure on Labour ministers**

Critics of the Labour leadership continued to make the point that in spite of the Beveridge furore, there was still little to show in terms of reconstruction. A leading exponent of this view was the socialist intellectual, Harold Laski.

Doctrinally, [Labour] is committed to securing great changes in the ownership of the means of production before the close of the war. . . . Its leaders make large promises about the building of a new world in which the workers shall enjoy that economic security and the standard of life which, as it claims, would follow upon the great changes. But the representatives of the Labour Party in Mr Churchill's government do not ask for any of the changes to which they are, like their followers, committed. They do not do so because they believe that Mr Churchill and his Conservative colleagues would reject their demands.

The leaders of the Labour Party are thus led to acquiesce in a policy which refuses to their doctrines the status of 'fundamentals' and they accept, as a result, methods of social organisation incompatible with the kind of society to which they are committed. They defend their attitude in different ways. 'National unity' must not be disturbed, in the interest of victory. . . . At the end of the war, they say, the nation can choose between Conservative policy and Socialist policy, though this view omits the vital fact that, at the end of the war, the impulse that gives agreement and consent their atmosphere of urgency will have largely become inoperative.

Or they urge that an attitude of 'give and take' is the implied condition of coalition government; and they point to a long list of social reforms, the 'guaranteed week', the increase in old age pensions, the virtual abolition of the means test, and so forth, which, in the absence of coalition, it would, in their opinion, have taken long years to achieve.

But if we seriously examine the character of the social reforms the Labour leaders have secured, it is clear that none of them presupposes any change in the relations of production while the Coalition Government lasts; and it is the central thesis of the Labour Party's doctrine that, in the absence of such changes before the end of the war, the fruits of victory will have been thrown away. There is, therefore, a decisive contradiction between the acts of Labour leaders and the principles of their party. The Labour leaders assist in the application of a policy which destroys the hope of achieving the ends to which they are formally committed.

Harold Laski, *Reflections on the Revolution of Our Time*, London, 1943, pp. 354–5.

4.14 The need for decisions

Attlee, Bevin and Morrison were in fact trying to push the Prime Minister towards greater activity, but constantly ran up against the Treasury view that Britain's post-war financial position was uncertain.

The most urgent need in the immediate post-war period will be to find a home and employment for all those who have served the country. Employers and workers in industry and agriculture will want to know where they stand. Builders of houses, schools and hospitals will be wanting to get work. All this involves taking definite decisions of policy. But no real progress can be made in shaping Government policy for the post-war period so long as we adhere to the principle that decisions involving financial commitments cannot be made until our post-war financial position is definitely known. Without a firm decision by the War Cabinet on the subjects which must be dealt with as matters of urgency for the reconstruction period, our plans must remain uncertain and nothing can be brought to the point of legislative enactment.

It is doubtful whether we shall, when hostilities end, be better placed than we are now to forecast financial burdens which the Government is capable of assuming. The uncertainties of world trade and military security will inevitably make the financial picture as much a matter of conjecture as it is today, but we cannot postpone definite action until these have been resolved. We refused to make definite decisions on the Beveridge Report without having considered other demands. The principle of refusing to make piecemeal decisions is sound, but the moral cannot possibly be to make no decisions at all.

Only one course remains and it is a reasonable one. It is for the Government to make now the best forecast it can of the financial and economic position of the country after the war and on that basis to take a major decision as to the items which it is prepared to carry through into law before the end of the war. . . .

Official plans are not enough, nor is the taking of decisions upon them 'in principle'. The subsequent work of preparing legislation takes considerable time, as the experience of the Beveridge Report is proving, and requires detailed decisions of policy. Parliamentary time is also needed. We urge, therefore, the taking of early decisions on reconstruction planning intended for wartime legislative implementation where necessary.

'The Need for Decisions', Memorandum by the Deputy Prime Minister, the Minister of Labour and National Service, and the Home Secretary, 26 June 1943, PRO PREM 4 87/8.

4.15 Proceeding with an education bill

During 1943 the one major reform given the go-ahead by ministers was an education bill, though Rab Butler was well aware that his colleagues had given their assent for some curious reasons.

I have been thinking over the back history of how the proposals for educational reform have managed to come to the front. As is usual in such manouevres, it has been partly by design and seizing opportunities, and partly by the fact that various circumstances created the opportunities.

At the Prime Minister's party shortly before the Recess (on 14th July), John Anderson said to me that he and the Chancellor had decided to back the education proposals, because they were not yet ready for Beveridge, and because they were conscientiously anxious about the effect of the full implementation of the Beveridge proposals upon the National Exchequer – and indeed upon the National character. . . .

As far as I am aware my colleagues have not been into the subject very deeply. Their reasons for plumping for an Education Bill are fortunately clothed in considerable forgetfulness of the revolutionary nature of educational change. They have been prompted to come the way of education because it has been very difficult to obtain agreement between the Parties on any matters which involve property or the pocket, whereas, on religious questions, there is a feeling that it is out-of-date to wrangle.[12] This is a further example of how political interest is shifting from the soul of man to his economic position, which all seems very unhealthy.

However, whether it is unhealthy or not, it certainly enables me to obtain considerable support for the Education proposals. The Prime Minister, I know from his views faithfully recorded to me, feels it will be possible to treat controversial parts of this Bill as non-political, and thus prevent a split between the major Parties. On the other hand, were the Government to press ahead with the Uthwatt

[12] Much of the debate about educational reform concerned the church schools: what should be the place of the voluntary bodies – notably the Anglican Roman Catholic churches – in the new state system?

Report,[13] they would find the question of Betterment coming to the front and, as it is, the new Minister of Planning is finding himself in very deep water.

It might have been possible to obtain a wider measure of agreement about the Beveridge Report had it not been produced in such an extraordinary way by one man, boosted by the Prime Minister's personal, confidential friend (the Minister of Information), and bruited abroad over the world by his vast office. The result has been that the Beveridge Plan has not marched hand in hand with that gentlemanly instinct which is so vital a feature of the Conservative Party, and without which the Conservative Party cannot be brought to undertake any reform. There is a feeling that Beveridge is a sinister old man, who wishes to give away a great deal of other people's money.

Diary notes by R. A. Butler, 9 Sep 1943: Butler papers, G15, ff. 81 and 90–1.

4.16 'New Men, New Measures?'

The introduction of educational reform was not sufficient to convince many commentators that reconstruction was being taken seriously, as this editorial demonstrates.

The unanswered question is the Government's intentions in post-war domestic policy; and the Government changes give at best only dusty answers. Like the policemen in the 'Pirates of Penzance', Ministers say in chorus 'We Go, We Go', but like Gilbert's constables again, they do not go; no visible headway is made. It has been suggested that the Prime Minister may take the opportunity, when Parliament reassembles, to announce a re-modelling of the system of Cabinet committees to facilitate decisions, as well as preparations, in matters of home reconstruction. The promotion of Mr Law, and its possible implications, suggest that a rationalisation of foreign policy to cover and collate all aspects may be envisaged, however dimly.[14]

[13] The findings of a committee under Mr Justice Uthwatt, established to consider some of the complex problems of town and country planning, particularly those of compensation and betterment.

[14] Richard Law had been promoted to become a Minister of State at the Foreign Office.

Can the same be said of home affairs? There is no evidence that it can. The machinery for canalising preparatory work and reaching conclusions already exists in the Home Affairs Committee of the Cabinet, and with its sub-committees on general reconstruction and the Beveridge proposals, now handed over by Sir John Anderson, who within the limits set has done excellent work, to Mr Attlee, who has a Ministerial reputation still to make. What it lacks is power to move; and in the present Government the starting signal can only come from one source, the Prime Minister. . . .

The Churchillian mode of government is on trial. Formal descriptions of the War Cabinet system, its committees and their articulation, tell much less than half the story. A great deal of hard and essential work is done by these means; but the first, middle and last words are spoken, or not spoken, elsewhere. The War Cabinet itself meets singularly seldom, and Ministers talk with their great leader, or indeed with one other, surprisingly rarely. The instrument of government, loaded with great war and post-war tasks, is splayed out like the prongs of a fork jabbed into granite. Worthy White Papers on education, the health services, workmen's compensation, pensions, social insurance, family allowances and the rest of the Beveridge proposals are, and will be, ably produced, ground work is laid upon ground work. But the question that matters most to the people of this country, the questions of highest policy – the prevention of want, the use and control of the land, the realities of demobilisation, industrial re-equipment, overseas trade policy, transport co-ordination, civil aviation, and social administration – all these must apparently remain without even interim replies, and certainly without legislative answers, so long as the voice of Downing Street cannot find time from its vast strategic exercises to speak or to choose a spokesman in its stead. Pertinently, Mr Doland MP asks in a letter to The Times:

> Are we to repeat the stupidities and inept gyrations of 1918, when no fewer than 196 committees dealing with post-war affairs were set up and the results were (to a very great extent) never acted upon?

'Have we not in this kingdom [the writer asks] a "Churchill" for home affairs?' Moses may not be able to come down from the mountain, but he may yet be able to send down the graven tablets by other hands.

The Economist, 2 October 1943.

4.17 Appointing a Minister of Reconstruction

One further move forward at the end of 1943 was the appointment of a minister responsible for co-ordinating reconstruction policy. As this extract from his autobiography shows, the man chosen by Churchill, Lord Woolton (at the time Minister of Food) was by no means keen to take on the task.

Towards the end of October 1943, the Prime Minister asked me to lunch with him and told me that he proposed to make me Minister of Reconstruction. I found the proposal unattractive. I told him that I realised that, contrary to usual practice, I had stayed at one Ministry for the whole period of my government service, but that as I did not propose to remain in Government when the war was over, I saw no point in making any change, unless he was dissatisfied with my conduct of affairs, in which case, of course, I would be glad to return to business life. It was a distressing interview. . . . I found myself very unwilling to accept the Prime Minister's suggestion, particularly as I saw that it would bring me into the range of political discussion and, in fact, party political disagreements. He told me, however, that this was the principal reason for inviting me to take the new post: I was an independent, belonging to no Party, and both the Conservative and Labour members of the Coalition Government had been consulted, and had agreed to serve on the Reconstruction Committee under my chairmanship: he said that I would be a member of the War Cabinet, and in charge of the home front.

I was still unconvinced and asked for time to consider it, but when the Prime Minister . . . told me that the King had been consulted and wanted me to do it, this, of course, prevented any further conversation on the matter. . . .

But the question was – what to do? My job was to try to get the concurrence of my colleagues to the blue-prints of post-war Britain, and the said colleagues were all grossly overworked with the problems of their own departments. . . .

Looking back to the conditions after the 1914–18 war, I came to the conclusion that the major post-war problem might well be that of unemployment. The Prime Minister, when he appointed me, visualised the problem of reconstruction as food, homes, and work. In order of importance I reversed them. I felt that if we could be sure of keeping people employed, then homes would follow and food would be provided, and the people would be able to pay for these services. . . .

In the Cabinet committee the major parties were equal in numbers, but there was a difference in their outlook. All knew that the coalition of parties in the Government would end. So powerful had been the dominance of Mr. Churchill during the war, and so obvious had been the hold that he had over the public, that I question whether any member of that committee believed that after the election was over the Labour Party would be in power. Consequently the Labour ministers, sincere in their belief in their Socialist principles, were not subject to the restraining force that they might be in office and have to carry out those plans. The Conservatives were more cautious. It was my function and my duty to get agreement between them. Each side was pressing to ensure that its own political principles were either preserved or advanced.

Lord Woolton, *The Memoirs of the Rt. Hon. the Earl of Woolton*, London, 1959, pp. 260–1, 265, 267 and 276.

4.18 **'The Body That Needed A Soul'**

David Low made the point that Woolton's appointment was desperately needed to inject real meaning into the reconstruction process. Jowitt, W. S. Morrison and Portal were all ministers hitherto struggling to push forward domestic reform.

David Low, 'The Body That Needed A Soul', *Evening Standard*, 12 November 1943.

4.19 Reconstruction and the future of coalition

With the end of the European war in sight after D-Day, incentives to coalition unity were gradually eroded, and social reform became entangled with the question of when an election would be called.

Tuesday 18th July: The post-war Reconstruction machine seems badly blocked again. I had hoped that when Woolton had got rid of Employment, Social Security, and Town and Country Planning, the way would be cleared for dealing with a lot of other questions, including many in my field. But we are getting no decisions and everyone, ministers and officials alike, seems to be dragging back and playing for position. No one ever says, 'Go ahead and God bless you'; everyone says, 'I haven't been consulted. Therefore nothing should be done.'

Tuesday 22nd August: Meeting of the Labour Party National Executive to consider (i) Conference arrangements and (ii) the publication of the statement agreed on at the last National Executive Meeting about the next general election. . . . Attlee says that he objects to saying publicly that we shall fight the next election as an independent party as much as he would object to saying that he has not become a Conservative. These things should be taken for granted. We then have a frank discussion as to how this Coalition Government should come to an end. Attlee thinks that after the German surrender we shall all be too busy for a little while to think about this, but that a moment will come when the P.M. will say to him that he hopes, having gone through the war in Europe together, we can go on together through a general election on an agreed programme. Attlee would then reply that he is afraid that this is impossible and that, when the general election comes . . . we must offer the country the choice between two alternative programmes. But, Attlee insists and all agree with him, we should aim at closing our association with the Conservatives, and particularly with the P.M., without any bitterness or ill-feeling and with expressions of mutual respect. . . . I say that I am sure this course is both morally right and politically wise, and this is the general view.

Pimlott (ed.), *Second World War Diary of Hugh Dalton*: entries for 18 July and 22 August 1944, pp. 769 and 779–80.

4.20 Deadlock over Town and Country Planning

After publishing white papers promising reform in the areas of health and employment, the coalition found it had run out of policy areas upon which left and right could agree. Instead of bold reform in town and country planning, the best ministers hoped for was to make provision for the acquistion and development of land for post-war planning purposes.

The temporary deadlock in the Committee stage of the Town and Country Planning Bill has a clear and well-marked genesis. Ever since the appearance of the recommendation by the Uthwatt Committee that compensation in respect of the public acquisition or public control of land should not exceed sums based on the standard of values at March 31, 1939, the Coalition Government have been confronted with the need to give precise legislative formulation to this seemingly straightforward but in reality intricate and momentous suggestion. The conditions under which they have had to perform the task were in a high degree difficult. In the first place, the conduct of the war not only pre-empted the major part of the Cabinet and the Prime Minister's attention but also imposed the fundamental request that coalition unity must not be endangered by preoccupation with major controversial questions. But compensation was precisely such a question. The views of the Labour and Conservative parties differed as sharply as they could on any political issue, the Left being in principle disposed to increasing public ownership of land, the Right to the maintenance of private ownership. In the second place, the technical details of the subject were considerable and again associated with differing political attitudes. The Coalition had to steer a course between the Scylla of a solution favouring land speculators and the Charybdis of one imposing undue hardship on great classes of property-owners. These are the circumstances that explain, though they don't excuse, the postponement of the Cabinet's decision from 1941 to 1944.

Decision is not easier now than it was then; it is more difficult. Indeed, the unity imposed on the Coalition three years ago by outside perils might have been turned to secure this most difficult agreement. Now that the danger presses less closely...the centrifugal pressure of dissimilar political views strains each stage of the discussion; and the temporary breakdown of the Planning Bill over its compensation clauses brings matters to a head.

The Times, 10 October 1944.

4.21 'Coalition and compromise'

Looking back as the coalition inexorably came to an end, this editorial could not help stressing how the high hopes of a brave new world had not been fulfilled.

Mr Churchill's invitation to men of 'every party and no party' to join him in a coalition, first in a 'caretaker' Government and later, after the General Election, in a re-formed National Government, has failed to evoke any response from the leaders of the major political parties. . . .

It would indeed be surprising if the Prime Minister's coalition call had met with any enthusiasm. It has created something like consternation in certain sections of the Conservative party, which are as eager to break with Labour as the Labour party's left wing is to break with them. There is no doubt where the Labour and Liberal parties, as parties, stand, whatever some of their leaders may feel privately. Their recent conferences committed them to withdraw from the Government and fight the election as independent parties. . . .

It is difficult to see what basis there could be for a durable all-party Government after the war with Germany. It is true, of course, that the Far Eastern war will call for continued national effort, but the Japanese collapse may come sooner than has been generally anticipated. It is also true that there will be vast national tasks of reconstruction and resettlement, and that the new Parliament will inherit a legacy of unfinished plans, a mountain of White Papers to be translated into Acts of Parliament. But Mr Churchill's words to the Conservative conference might be paraphrased: 'Never was there a time when so much was planned and projected with so little hope of being turned from paper into action.' The delay in completing social insurance plans; the failure to reach an agreement on land values, without which no town planning is possible; the housing muddle; the coal calamity – these are the fruits of coalition in domestic affairs, the inhibiting effects of the fear of producing controversy. The coalition is getting more and more threadbare. . . .

Dilute compromise may be a necessary ingredient of domestic politics in wartime, but it would be a disaster as a permanent principle. The last twelve months have amply illustrated – if illustration were needed – the severe brake that is put on any practical progress by the necessity of attempting to reconcile the irreconcilable. The only hope of being able to confront with any success the vast problems of the post-war years is to have a Government that knows its mind and has a policy.

'Coalition and compromise', *The Economist*, 24 March 1945.

5

Popular politics in wartime

How and why did British public opinion swing to the left in the war years? With hindsight, it becomes clear that the pre-1939 ascendancy of the Conservative party collapsed under the impact of total war, with its demands for equality of sacrifice and sweeping controls over all aspects of civilian life. But at the time, the existence of an electoral truce and a coalition government made it difficult to gauge the public mood. The extracts in this chapter highlight some of the confusing signals. On the one hand, there were clear manifestations of radical opinion, such as crushing by-election defeats for Tory candidates at the hands of independents and the left-wing Common Wealth party. For many commentators, however, there was a more important force at work from the summer of 1940 onwards. Surely Churchill, the great war leader and national saviour, could not be beaten at any post-war election?

5.1 Priestley's Postscripts

The popular mood of 1940 was captured in a famous series of radio broadcasts by the Yorkshireman J. B. Priestley. His last broadcast on 20 October hinted at behind-the-scenes pressure on the BBC to put an end to his controversial calls for change.

As many of you will remember, I began these postscripts just after Dunkirk; got going with them during those blazing summer weeks when France collapsed and we were threatened with immediate invasion, and world opinion began to think we were doomed. We knew very well that we weren't doomed, and our people began to show the world what stuff they're made of, and the sight was glorious.

Throughout those weeks as the spirits of the British people rose, to the bewilderment and secret concern of the Nazis, who couldn't understand such behaviour, many of us felt that here now was a country capable, not only of defying and then defeating the Nazis and Fascists, but capable too of putting an end to the world that produced Nazis and Fascists; capable of working a miracle, the miracle of man's liberation. . . .

Stupid persons have frequently accused me in public of . . . taking advantage of my position to bring party politics into my talks. This is extremely ironical because I am not a member of any political party. . . . It's not I, but they, who put party before country, for I've never even learnt to think in terms of a political party. And the most I've asked for in these talks is that we should mean what we say; be really democratic, for example, while fighting for democracy; and that we should make some attempt to discover the deeper causes of this war and to try and find a remedy for them, thus making this a colossal battle, not only against something, but also for something positive and good. If all this, together with certain obvious elements of social justice and decency seems to you Socialism, Communism or Anarchy, then you are at liberty to call me a Socialist, a Communist or an Anarchist, though I would implore you to stop merely pasting on labels and instead to think a little. . . .

I think it's true to say that at the present time this country of ours, because of its courage and its proud defiance, its determination to put an end to this international brigandage and racketeering of the Hitlers and Mussolinis and their riff-raff is the hope of all that is best in the world, which watches us with admiration. But our greatest potential ally is not this power or that, but the growing hope in decent folk everywhere that civilisation can be saved; . . . that a reasonable liberty along with a reasonable security can be achieved; that democracy is not an experiment that was tried and failed, but a great creative force that must now be released again. If we can make all these things plain to the world by the way in which we now order our lives here, then I don't believe this will even be a long war – the daylight will come soon and all these evil apparitions from the night of men's bewilderment and despair will vanish, but if apathy and stupidity return to reign once more; if the privileges of a few are seen to be regarded as more important than the happiness of many; if a sterile obstruction is preferred to creation; if our faces are still turned towards the past instead of towards the future; if too many of us will simply not trouble to know, or if we do know, will not care, then the great opportunity will pass us by, and soon the light will be going out again.

J. B. Priestley, *Postscripts*, London, 1940, pp. 96–100.

5.2 Popular attitudes to wartime politics

This report by Mass-Observation confirmed that party politics had been pushed into the background by the threat of invasion and the existence of a coalition government. At the same time, there were already signs that the pre-war political order was being undermined.

People do not, for the most part, feel themselves personally involved in political problems. Politics is something outside everyday life, just as religion is outside the everyday life of three-quarters of the population. Political and news subjects compose only a minute fraction of ordinary conversation; and several surveys have shown astonishing proportions of people who do not know who are the key Cabinet Ministers or the name of their local M.P. This position has been reaffirmed this month, when under half of those questioned in London had any idea of the name of their local M.P.

The easiest way in which people interest themselves in politics, is, however, in personalities. But this is not necessarily politics in the democratic sense. Chamberlain was for a long time an interest[ing] topic, largely because he was the leader of the country. Antagonism became violent towards him, but not his Party, when he appeared to have let the country down. Now Churchill fills the same place, though with appreciably more popularity (Chamberlain never reached as high as 80% in favour). . . .

The popularity of this Prime Minister is exceptionally high, but there are signs that it has not increased in recent weeks. It has been suggested that one reason for this is the acceptance of the leadership of the Conservative Party. Investigations show that rather more than one person in ten did feel that his acceptance of this leadership was a bad thing. On the other hand, five times as many people, including in Labour areas, felt that it was a good thing. . . .

It is often said that the effect of no by-elections and a lull in Party politics is to reduce the general level of political feeling, and there is some support for this from the statistics of elections after the last Great War. . . . Pursuing the same theme, detailed verbatim conversations indicated that on the whole most people had not changed their particular political views. This was also confirmed in some direct questioning, where only one person in ten said that their views had been changed. . . . The few who had changed their Party, mostly had become Labour. There are other distinct signs of a tendency towards socialism, often unconscious, in the minds of persons previously or still regarding themselves as Conservative. But the more significant trend, which cannot be expressed in figures . . . is a trend towards uncertainty and questioning of the status quo. . . .

The feeling that the world is in the melting pot, cannot be said to have yet fully impacted on the mass of people. But the feeling of doubt and uncertainty about the future is probably higher today than it has been for a very long time past in this country. The upper and middle-classes feel this more than the working-classes. Men are much more aware of it than women. But in the last few months it has been hard to find, even among women, many who do not unconsciously regard this war as in some way revolutionary, or radical.

Mass-Observation Typescript Report No. 496, 'Popular attitudes to wartime politics', 20 November 1940: Mass-Observation Archive, University of Sussex.

5.3 **Wartime by-elections: the case of Dunbartonshire**

Mass-Observation was incorrect to state there were 'no by-elections'. Under an electoral truce, Conservative and Labour leaders agreed that a candidate proposed by the incumbent party would not be opposed, but this did not prevent others from contesting seats as they became available. The case of Dunbartonshire, reported on here by the Ministry of Information, shows that the electoral truce was unpopular with local activists from early on in the war.

(1) Polling on February 27th resulted:
McKinlay (Lab.) 21,900
McEwen (Com.) 3,862

(2) 25,700 of an electorate of about 67,000 (nominal, perhaps 45,000 effective) polled. This was a higher poll than the last by-election, in Northampton, when approximately 30% voted.

(3) The poll was the highest yet scored by a Communist since the war, and the first time a Communist candidate did not forfeit his deposit.

(4) Labour fought on a Labour Party platform and Conservative co-operation was not apparent either in meetings or in election literature. It is estimated, however, that the votes cast for McKinlay contain some thousands from Unionists,[1] Liberals and Nationalists.

(5) The constituency has few natural unities, either of geography or of social class. It contains the Vale of Leven, 'the reddest strip of Britain', a large new housing estate (Knightswood) for which the Labour candidate has been largely responsible, and considerable middle and upper class residential areas (Helensburgh). The area has been virtually untouched by evacuation, but much influenced by difficulties in industrial relations on Clydeside. . . .

(6) Although the constituency has suffered little from direct impacts of the war (no raids), there are a number of real grievances widely felt. In the industrial field economic class distinctions are strongly felt, the provision of welfare facilities is noticeably poor, transport for workers is extremely bad, and common talk contains persistent allegations about inefficient management, supply muddles and lack of supervision in key places. There is a strong local grievance that the Minister of Aircraft Production has not thought it worth while to visit the area. On the day before polling there was a lockout of shipyard workers which aroused violent feelings over the whole industrial area. . . .

(8) McKinlay's policy was very simple: 'behind Churchill' and 'against the Reds'.

(9) McEwens's policy . . . was mainly the exploitation of grievances: profiteering, rationing, A[ir] R[aid] P[recautions] and shelters, growing Fascism in Britain, self-determination for India. Several of these points failed to arouse interest and were soon dropped, e.g. India, A.R.P. . . .

(10) An observers' study of the campaign showed that the size of the Communist vote was felt by those on the spot to be an advance for the C.P. It would also appear that the Communists succeeded in

[1] Another term for Tory supporters, deriving from the name Conservative and Unionist party.

mobilising more goodwill than was reflected in the actual vote. In election discussions people heard expressing sympathy for the point of view put forward by the Communist candidate remained unconvinced that the Communists in any way represented an alternative Government. The vagueness of their general arguments was commented upon and it was frequently remarked that they were ill-adjusted to local Scottish conditions. Lack of Conservative support for the Labour candidate caused some surprise and promoted discussions about 'the unreality of Government unity'.

(11) The general conclusion of our report is that a situation of some danger is revealed and that a close watch ought to be kept on developments in this area.

'Dunbartonshire by-election', Home Intelligence Report, 5 March 1941, PRO INF 1/292.

5.4 'England your England'

Notwithstanding any increased sympathy for the Communist party, many writers were struck by the public's partriotic response to the war. In the first of a series of 'Searchlight Books', published early in 1941, George Orwell reflected on the profound impact of the momentous events of 1940.

I have spoken all the while of 'the nation', 'England', 'Britain', as though forty-five million souls could somehow be treated as a unit. But is not England notoriously two nations, the rich and the poor? Dare one pretend that there is anything in common between people with £100,000 a year and people with £1 a week?. . . . It is quite true that the so-called races of Britain feel themselves to be very different from one another. A Scotsman, for instance, does not thank you if you call him an Englishman. . . .

Economically, England is certainly two nations, if not three or four. But at the same time the vast majority of the people feel themselves to be a single nation and are conscious of resembling one another more than they resemble foreigners. Patriotism is usually stonger than class-hatred, and always stronger than any kind of internationalism. . . . In England patriotism takes different forms in different classes, but it runs like a connecting thread through nearly all of them. . . . In all countries the poor are more national than the rich, but the English working class are outstanding in their abhorrence of foreign habits. Even when they are obliged to live abroad for years they refuse either to accustom themselves to foreign food or to learn foreign languages. Nearly every Englishman of working-class origin considers it effeminate to pronounce a foreign word correctly. During the war of 1914–18 the English working class were in contact with foreigners to an extent that is rarely possible. The sole result was that they brought back a hatred of all Europeans, except the Germans, whose courage they admired. In four years on French soil they did not even acquire a liking for wine. . . .

Up to a point, the sense of national unity is a substitute for a 'world-view'. Just because patriotism is all but universal and not even the rich are uninfluenced by it, there can be moments when the whole nation suddenly swings together and does the same thing, like a herd of cattle facing a wolf. There was such a moment, unmistakably, at the time of the disaster in France. After eight months of wondering what the war was about, the people suddenly knew what they had got to do: first, to get the army away from Dunkirk, and secondly to prevent invasion. It was like the awakening of a giant. Quick! Danger! The Philistines be upon thee, Samson! And then the swift unanimous action – and then, alas, the prompt relapse into sleep. In a divided nation that would have been exactly the moment for a big peace movement to arise. . . .

England is the most class-ridden country under the sun. It is a land of snobbery and privilege, ruled largely by the old and silly. But in any calculation about it one has got to taken into account its emotional unity, the tendency of nearly all its inhabitants to feel alike and act together in moments of supreme crisis. It is the only great country in Europe that is not obliged to drive hundreds of thousands of its nationals into exile or the concentration camps. At this moment, after a year of war, newspapers and pamphlets abusing the Government, praising the enemy and clamouring for surrender are being sold on the streets, almost without interference. And this is less from a respect for freedom of speech than from a simple perception that these things don't matter. It is safe to let a paper like *Peace News* be sold, because it is certain that ninety-five per cent of the population will never want to read it. The nation is bound together by an invisible chain. At any normal time the ruling class will rob, mismanage, sabotage, lead us into the muck; but let popular opinion really make itself heard, let them get a tug from below that they cannot avoid feeling, and it is difficult not to respond.

George Orwell, *The Lion and the Unicorn: Socialism and the English Genius*, London, 1941, reprinted in S. Orwell and I. Angus (eds), *The Collected Essays, Journalism and Letters of George Orwell*, Vol. 2, London, 1977 edn., pp. 83–8.

5.5 Home-made socialism

By early 1942, with the war still going badly, Ministry of Information observers were finding clear indications of a swing to the left in political attitudes throughout most parts of the country.

In view of a reference in our Weekly Report No. 72 to the spread of 'a kind of home-made socialism' among certain sections of the public, Regional Information Officers were asked whether any similar trends of opinion had been noticed in their Regions. They were particularly requested not to make special enquiries into this subject, but merely to report any spontaneous evidence of these trends. . . .

The material which follows summarises the main points from the R[egional] I[information] O[fficer]s reports.

Northern Region: 'The bias in popular political thought seems to be turning from liberty to equality'. Though many people feel that they are working for the community rather than for their own gain, they are, at the same time, doubtful of an equally altruistic spirit among their employers, who are suspected of resisting changes which might effect their post-war profits. . . .

North Eastern Region: Here it seems that 'there is a more apparent leaning towards socialism since Russia became an Ally'. Successful Soviet resistance and 'the ruthless spread of Russia's dictatorship' are contrasted with our own constant failures and 'bureaucratic procrastination'. 'Inequalities of sacrifice and reward apparent in our own system' are also said to increase this leaning towards socialism.

This, it is pointed out, does not represent an 'organised political feeling', but rather an outlet for the urge to get on with the war effort.

North Midland Region: 'It is agreed', says the R.I.O., 'that there is a strong tendency towards the ideal of socialism in all classes'. Once again this is said to be mainly non-political.

The following factors are suggested as causes of this tendency:

(a) A levelling-up of classes, resulting from bombing and rationing.
(b) The Russian successes.
(c) The blaming of vested interests for 'ills of production'.
(d) The fear that conditions of the last post-war period may be repeated. . . .

London Region: During the last six months it is believed that 'a new trend of opinion' has gained impetus and is now said to be 'growing like a jungle plant'. 'During the earlier part of the war, socialism developed among people who, thrown out of their normal circumstances, were more in contact with the poorer classes'. But more recently it appears to have increased considerably 'among black-coated workers who are said to be reading and discussing a great deal'. The 'employer class', as well as those who formerly always voted conservative, are also 'turning to this idea'. Many of them appear to feel that socialism is inevitable, and are resigned to the prospect, as it is agreed that 'better social opportunities for everyone and improved conditions must come'. . . .

Southern Region: No similar trends of opinion have been noticed in this area, but the R.I.O. mentions a growing tendency 'to speculate as to whether our Parliamentary system will be able to function much longer'. He alludes to 'a lot of talk about its being out of date', and suggests the possibility that the 'cult for Cripps may be due to a sort of sub-conscious reversion to the Cromwell idea – an austere but democratic dictator'.

South Western Region: A distinct swing to what is vaguely called 'the Left' is reported from this Region. It does not appear to be on Labour Party or socialist lines, but it does seem to be directed against the Conservative Party insofar as this represents the so-called 'Men of Munich', the 'old gang', 'Colonel Blimp' and similar diehard types. For this feeling it is believed that the continued opprobrium of Press and Parliament are partly responsible. . . .

Scottish Region: While it is stated that 'nothing so definite as a group is growing up' political consciousness in this Region seems to be increasing. The three orthodox parties have either 'fallen from grace' or are making no headway, and attention is drawn to the 'awakening' of the Communist Party, since Russia's entry into the war; it is reported that 'over 1200 new members enrolled during the first six weeks of this year'. . . .

South Eastern Region: In the urban and industrial areas of this Region an 'inclination to think socially' is said to exist among people who have hitherto never 'embraced political socialism'. Vested interests, and 'string-pulling behind the scenes' are said to have aroused fairly widespread complaint, and 'there is a belief that our failure to reach a 100 per cent war effort is attributable to them'. . . .

It is, however, questioned whether, in many rural areas of this Region any real desire exists for a complete change in the social order. In these areas, respect for 'the parson, the doctor and the old families who are all part and parcel of the locality' is still apparent.

Conclusion: It will be seen that nothing so definite as an organised political movement can be said to underlie these reported tendencies. They seem mainly to spring from dissatisfaction with 'the lack of Government leadership; hence there arises a groping towards an unofficial and non-party type of social policy'. . . . One thing is apparently agreed by all: that there must and will be 'alterations in the present order of society'.

'Home-made socialism', Report by Home Intelligence Division, 24 March 1942, PRO INF 1/292.

5.6 The rise of the independents

Another indicator of public disaffection in the spring of 1942 was the vulnerability of Conservative candidates to by-election challenges from independent candidates, free from the constraints of the electoral truce. Here W. J. Brown, a former member of the Labour party, recounts how he swept to victory at the Rugby by-election.

The war was going badly, and by no means all of the defeats and disasters which befell us were attributable to our initial unpreparedness. So I had written an article for the *Sunday Pictorial*, entitled 'Wanted – Fifty Men of Courage', in which I appealed for brave and independent-minded men to come forward at by-elections and fight on their own feet, in defiance of the political truce which was muzzling the electorate. . . .

When I arrived back in England [from a visit to the United States] I resolved to fight a by-election. I looked at a number of seats as they fell vacant, but again and again was deterred from standing because some one else had jumped in first. On one occasion – Grantham – a powerful local candidate had emerged in the peson of Mr. W. D. Kendall, who in fact scored the first Independent victory of the war by winning the seat. On other occasions Mr. Pemberton Billing[2] was ahead of me. . . . When Rugby fell vacant, owing to the promotion of Captain Margesson to the House of Lords, I looked at that, but again Pemberton Billing got in first.

I had put Rugby out of my mind and was wondering when, if ever, circumstances would enable me to get in a serious political contest, when late one Saturday night I was informed on the telephone that Pemberton Billing was withdrawing from the Rugby contest. . . . It was unlikely, I judged, if my candidature were at once announced publicly, that another Independent candidate would emerge before nomination day, so that I should get a straight fight with the Conservative nominee. True, there was a Conservative majority of 8000-odd to destroy. True, the Conservative machine was reputedly the best in the country (had not Margesson been for years the Chief Whip of the Conservative Party?). True, I had never been in the town in my life and didn't know a soul in the place. . . . But all these things were incitements, not deterrents. On the instant I made up my mind to fight Rugby. . . .

I worked with tremendous energy throughout the contest, usually spending about seven hours a day in the car, and using the microphone, in addition to writing my own leaflets, and doing anything up to four meetings in the evening. Before long it became plain that we were making progress, and the enemy became increasingly perturbed. The Prime Minister sent a letter of support to my opponent, and so his supporters used the slogan: 'Vote for Holbrook – the man whom Churchill wants!' which I capped with the counter-slogan: 'Vote for Brown, the man whom Churchill *needs*'!. . . .

[2] Noel Pemberton Billing, who contested several by-elections as an independent. In the words of Paul Addison, he was a 'lone throw-back to the jingoism of the First World War', campaigning for 'reprisals against German air action, and victory by bombing alone. Travelling in a yellow Rolls-Royce, and bellowing out the cry of vengeance, Billing also introduced into his campaigns a general anti-Tory note, stressing Conservative misdeeds, and the need for full employment in peacetime' – *The Road to 1945*, p. 155.

On the day after the poll, I did not go to the count until half-past twelve, by which time I judged it would be nearly completed. . . . The figures were read out, and I was declared elected. . . . I went back to my hotel to hear the news that, simultaneously with my victory at Rugby, another Independent, George Reakes, had won Wallasey. . . .

I need not conceal that I felt the livliest satisfaction at the result of the Rugby battle. Never did a candidate give fewer pledges to his constituents. I gave only two: first, that I would speak and vote in the House on the merits of the case as I saw them; and second, that I would report back to the constituency . . . on my political activities. So that the result could not be attributed to demagogic promises on my part. I had wiped out with a margin of 700 to spare a Conservative majority of 8000. I had, without a machine, stood up to and beaten a combination of all the machines.

W. J. Brown, *So Far*, London, 1943, pp. 244–9.

5.7 The rise of Common Wealth

The first half of 1943 saw the emergence of a new force in British politics. Common Wealth consisted mainly of middle class, left-wing idealists; by pledging itself to social reforms such as the Beveridge Report, the party scored its first by-election success over the Conservative candidate at Eddisbury.

There have been twelve by-elections in Great Britain (excluding Northern Ireland) since the beginning of 1943. These elections, and their results, have been as follows:

Election	**Government candidates**	**Common Wealth**	**Independent candidates**
Hamilton	10,725		2503
Welsh University	3098	1330	
			755
			634
			101
King's Lynn	10,696		9027
Ashford (Kent)	9648	4192	
*Bristol	5867	4308	630
			258

*Watford	13839	11838	
Midlothian	11620	10751	
*Eddisbury	7537	8023	2803
*Daventry	9043	6591	4093
Hartlepools	13333	3634	2531 1510
*Newark	10120	3189	7110 2473
Aston	6316	1886	514

Notes: Government Candidates all Conservatives except Labour at Hamilton and Liberal at Welsh Universities. Candidate at Bristol entered as 'Common Wealth' was an Independent with C-W support (Jennie Lee).[3]

*Covered by M[ass]-O[bservation].

Thus in 12 by–Elections, the total votes polled have been as follows:

Government candidates	111,842
Common Wealth	54,412
Other candidates	36,272

With these votes, there have been returned one Common Wealth Member and eleven Government members (nine Conservatives, one Liberal, and one Labour).

Common Wealth first contested the Ashford by-election, and have put up a candidate at every election since that date. Common Wealth polls show a steady rise up to Watford, and an uninterrupted decline since that date. . . .

It may be taken that a vote against the government candidate of anything between 45 and 60% is normal. In only four of the twelve elections did the anti-government candidate vote fail to reach 45%, and it is unfortunate that none of these four elections . . . was covered by M-O observers. . . .

Mass-Observation has been asked on several occasions, what was the reason for the exceptionally high Common Wealth vote at Eddisbury. It is of course easy to give a reason in the fact that the C-W canvassing in Eddisbury was very much more thorough and very much quicker off the mark than it has been in any other by-election. But this is not the whole story. For the percentage of the total vote cast for Common Wealth in Eddisbury was not exceptional. It amounted to 44%, a figure exceeded at Watford and at Midlothian (46% and 48% respectively).

[3] Wife of Aneurin Bevan.

And yet the first explanation, – that of the thoroughness of Common Wealth canvassing at Eddisbury, – is probably the correct one. For it is easier to poll a high vote without the presence of additional independent candidates than it is with one. There are fewer issues which have to be made plain to the electorate.

Mass-Observation Typescript Report No. 1844, 'By-elections, February–June 1943', 16 June 1943: Mass-Observation Archive, University of Sussex.

5.8 The movement back to party

In spite of isolated successes for independents and Common Wealth, a more significant feature of by-elections was the way in which local activists, especially in the Labour party, were unwilling to back the 'official' candidate. The grudging attitude of Labour in the example below, one of many as the war progressed, led a local newspaper editorial to describe the electoral truce as a 'dead letter'.

Viscount Suirdale, National government candidate, had a majority of 1,086 over Mr Sam Bennett, Independent Socialist in the Peterborough by-election. . . .

Lord Suirdale, thanking his supporters, said he regarded his election as a victory for Mr Churchill and for the electors who had decided to put first things first and concentrate upon winning the war, leaving political issues until afterwards. It had been a good, clean fight. He admired greatly the courage, cleanness and fairness with with Mr Bennett had fought and could not have wished for a better opponent.

Until the next election, and, he hoped, for a long time afterwards, he was to be the Member of Parliament for Peterborough. He stood as a National Government candidate on a non-party basis, and it would be his endeavour to represent everybody, irrespective of political label. . . .

Mr Bennett said that, while he believed that the war must be fought to a finish, and that all must concentrate on that, there must also be a concentration on peace problems. He was convinced that the Conservative party, with their usual unreadiness, would be found unready for peace.

'Lord Suirdale, like all the other Conservatives, had cashed in on the popularity of Winston Churchill, the man they kept out of Government for 20 years'.

There were cheers from a small part of the crowd at this, and cries of 'No, no!'. Mr Bennett added that it had been a good, clean fight and he had enjoyed it. When the boys came home, there would be a different result. . . .

Lord and Lady Suirdale went round to the Cecil Rooms, where they were given a rousing reception. Lord Exeter congratulated the new member on his victory and commended him on his hard work to secure it. Transport and black-out difficulties and the absence of many members of the organisation had meant a great deal more work for the candidate and for all who had worked with him in the cause of unity and in support of Mr Churchill. They were somewhat disappointed that there should be a by-election at all, but there was absolutely no doubt about the verdict of the Peterborough division. . . .

Born in 1902, Viscount Suirdale was educated at Winchester and Magdalen College, Oxford. For some years he was associated with the merchant banking firm of Grace Brothers & Co. Ltd, and then he became a partner in Reed & Brigstock, brokers on the Stock Exchange. . . .

The 'Standard' learns from one high up in Labour counsels that it is considered most unlikely that Mr Bennett, having resigned his Labour Party membership as well as his candidature, will attempt to seek reinstatement. That being so, it is expected that the Divisional Executive of the Labour Party will very soon be making a move, if not actually to select a candidate, at least to prepare the ground.

Peterborough Standard, 22 October 1943.

5.9 Party Prospects

Signs of an anti-Conservative trend at by-election contests were not considered sufficient in the eyes of some commentators to suggest that Labour was now on course for electoral victory. Above all, Churchill's popularity as war leader appeared to give the Tories the edge.

Several arguments are put forward, most of them negative in character, for the belief that the Conservative Party has, for the time at any rate, had its day. The most frequently heard argument, perhaps, is the suggestion that its tenure of office must end soon precisely because it has been long drawn out; the pendulum, it is argued, must swing at last the more so because the swing has been delayed. A second argument is that of what may be called war guilt. It was the Conservative Party, it is pointed out, that allowed Germany to grow strong. . . . A third argument . . . is that the Conservative Party, despite the large contribution which it has made to progressive legislation and administration during the past three-quarters of a century, is in essence reactionary. The pronounced policy of those who count most in its constitution thus serve as a brake on the wheel, not to oppose progress, but to infuse it with the utmost caution; and it is argued that this mentality is incapable of satisfying the present desire for broad forward moves in social and economic policy, carried through with boldness and innovation. . . .

The arguments against this thesis are at least equally numerous. In the first place, the fact that the pendulum has not swung for two decades is as much a reason for wondering whether it will swing even now as it is for assuming that it must swing. Secondly, there is Mr Churchill – and the fact that, whatever the war guilt of those who supported Mr Chamberlain, it is the present Government, led by the leader of the Conservative Party and backed by a Conservative Parliament, that will have won the war. At any rate, it is probable that, whatever party ultimately secures the balance of advantage in post-war politics, Mr Churchill, still leader of the Conservative Party, will win the first election after the war. This will almost certainly be the case, whether the first election is a coupon election or not. In any event, it will be a khaki election; the voting will be taken, not on the Uthwatt Report, but on the victorious conclusion of Britain's biggest war. . . . The outcome of the second and third elections after the war depends . . . first, on the actual successes or failures of the first post-war administrations, which may be mainly Conservative; and, secondly, on the ability of the Labour Party to convince the electors that, put in sole charge of the nation's affairs, it will have the ability to satisfy the nation's needs and aspirations more effectively.

Thus, the ultimate answer to the post-war political riddle lies in the constitution and development of the Labour Party rather than in that of the Conservative Party. . . . To rely upon such an unlikely event as the splitting of the Conservative Party after the war would be futile. There is, and has been, a distinct fissure within the Conservative Party between what may be called the Chamberlainites and the rest. Between Munich and the outbreak of war it was wide open, but it was covered, though not healed, when Mr Churchill – the only man who could have formed an effective third party – undertook the leadership of the party as well as the leadership of the nation. This will be by no means the first time that the Conservative Party has held firmly together despite a marked division within its ranks. . . . Moreover, the circumstances of wartime coalition have revealed a fissure, probably as large, within the Labour Party itself, not merely between the trade unions and the constituencies, but between those who believe in the policy of the coalition and those who distrust it. . . .

Will the Labour Party at last be able in the next decade to take the opportunity which has been open but not taken ever since the end of the last war? In other words, can it capitalise the popular desire for a dynamic advance in democratic politics? Can it prove itself, in practice as well as precept, less cautious than the Conservative Party, less sceptical and less mentally indisposed to the boldness that is the highest from of realism in politics? In short, can it win elections?

The Economist, 28 August 1943.

5.10 **Common Wealth success at Skipton**

During early 1944 the Conservatives suffered two humiliating by-election losses, the first in one of its traditional agricultural heartlands.

Sunday 9 January The Common Wealth candidate has won the by-election in the Skipton Division of Yorkshire by 221 votes. This is an unexpected blow to the Tories especially as Joe Toole, ex-Lord Mayor of Manchester and former Labour M.P. for Salford South, stood as an Independent & received 3,029 votes, not quite enough to save his deposit.[4] *The Times* on Wednesday said: 'The Conservative & National Govt. candidate has practically all the advantages &

[4] The full result was H. M. Lawson (Common Wealth) 12,222 votes, H. Riddiough (Conservative) 12,001, J. Toole (Independent) 3,029.

should retain this traditionally Conservative seat.' No other paper, as far as I could follow, indicated that the seat was in danger. Toole has been expelled from the Manchester Labour Party for breaking the electoral truce, which a number of Labour voters also violated. . . . Any R[oman] C[atholic] votes in the Divn. presumably went to Toole who is one of them. It is to be expected that the farmers, angry with Hudson,[5] asked themselves who of the two anti-Govt. candidates was most likely to win and voted for him. It is significant that the two Common Wealth successes have been gained in rural constituencies.

Tuesday 11 January A.J. Cummings has the adjoining comment on Skipton in his *News Chronicle* 'Spotlight'.[6] The old adage: 'If you win, praise the Agent; if you lose, blame the candidate', is being very vigorously applied in this instance. This particular candidate seems to have been a typical Yorkshire product. I imagine the Tory Party will be concerned at their loosening hold on the agricultural seats.

Jefferys (ed.) *Chuter Ede Diary*, p. 162.

5.11 The West Derbyshire by-election

Skipton was followed closely by defeat for the Tories at West Derbyshire – perhaps the most celebrated of all wartime by-elections.

The West Derby division has been traditionally held by the family of the Duke of Devonshire. The resigning member was a Colonel Hunloke, who was rumoured to have been 'keeping it warm' until Lord Hartington was old enough to become an M.P. He resigned because he was on active service outside England, and thought the constitutuency should have a representative who could represent it in the House. It was pointed out by some constituents that Lord Hartington was also a serving officer, and would be no more able to represent the constituency in the House than Colonel Hunloke was. . . .

[5] R. S. Hudson, Minister of Agriculture, was unpopular with farmers for refusing to raise prices to match pay increases awarded to farm labourers.

[6] The writer Cummings contrasted the youthful imagination of the Common Wealth candidate with the poor showing of his elderly Conservative rival.

The result of the polling on Feb. 17th 1944 was:

C. F. White (Ind)	16,336
Lord Hartington (Cons)	11,775
R. Goodall (Ind)	233
Majority	4,561

Charlie White. A burly, red-faced, white-haired man of about 53. Very well known in the neighbourhood, an Alderman of the County Council, Labour candidate at the last by-election. He resigned from the Labour Party and gave up his job as Matlock's Food Executive Officer to fight the election. His father had been a cobbler in the neighbourhood and had been returned to parliament in 1918 in opposition to another member of the Cavendish family. White was very well known and well liked in the district, particularly for acting on behalf of local working people, taking up individual pension cases, etc., and benefited also from his father's good reputation. . . .

Lord Hartington. Lord Hartington was the son of the Duke of Devonshire, a junior Minister, and Lord Lieutenant of the County. . . . Lord Hartington was 26, and had served in the army for five years in which he held a commission as a regular officer. He was fairly good looking and had a megaphonic voice. His speeches were very short, which suggested that he had been told not to say much in case he put his foot in it. This he did once or twice, notably when he is reported to have said that he thought the mines were already nationalised. . . .

Robert Goodall. Goodall was an unusual candidate even for a wartime election. A farm bailiff aged 27, he certainly had no money to spare, and it was said that his father mortgaged most of his property in order to raise the deposit. But Goodall held only one meeting in the market place, had no committee rooms, election address, posters, agent, or so far as could be seen, any policy. . . .

The election was in effect a straight fight between White and Hartington, and was largely carried out on the basis of personalities, particularly on White's side. For example, he brought up the fact that Lord Hartington's grandfather had turned the family estates into a company to escape death duties, to which Hartington replied after consulting his father, that this was a legal thing to do, and what was wrong with it. . . .

So far as the national press was concerned, the most outstanding feature of the campaigns was the fact that the majority of White's canvassing was done by a staff of Common Wealth workers from outside the constituency. There were said to be 80 of these, one of whom, a Russian, caused some amusement. She was a music hall actress who took time off for the election. It was said to be due to the efficiency of this team – often termed the 'Common Wealth Circus' – that White got in. . . .

According to one resident, the issue at stake was not whose policy was best, but whether people preferred the Cavendishes or the Whites. The personalities introduced into the election have already been referred to. Hartington gave very little in the way of policy, beyond standing for unity and support of Churchill.

Mass-Observation Typescript Report No. 2036, 'West Derby Bye-election, February 1944', 1 August 1944: Mass-Observation Archive, University of Sussex.

5.12 Churchill's reaction to the West Derbyshire defeat

The Prime Minister was naturally cast down by the defeat of a Conservative nominee in what had been – in view of White's pedigree – the closest yet to an open contest between the two main parties.

After lunch the results of the West Derbyshire by-election came through: Lord Hartington lost to Mr White, the Independent, by 4,500 votes. This caused a pall of the blackest gloom to fall on the P.M., who is personally afflicted by this emphatic blow to the Government in view of the *verbosa et grandis epistola* which he wrote to Hartington, in which he lauded the political record of the Cavendish family. Moreover there was trouble at Brighton a fortnight ago when he wrote another long letter and, in the event, Teeling, the Government candidate, only scraped home in the safest of Tory seats.

Sitting in his chair in his study at the Annexe, the P.M. looked old, tired and very depressed and was even muttering about a General Election. Now, he said, with great events pending, was the time when national unity was essential: the question of annihilating great states had to be faced: it began to look as if democracy had not the persistence necessary to go through with it, however well it might have shown capacity for defence.

Colville, *Fringes of Power*: diary entry for 18 February 1944

5.13 Who'll win?

In spite of West Derbyshire, political commentators continued to assume that Churchill would win any post-war election. One notable exception – which pointed the way towards the eventual result of the 1945 election – was an article written by Tom Harrisson, who tried to draw together the threads of evidence available in 1943 for an article published in 1944.

Because the Right was quiet in 1940 and 1941, dark years when all men's good will was need for survival, many leftward minds seem to have assumed a change of heart to match the tongue. . . . Belatedly, the left are having to recognise that their future fight may be tough. That Social change which 1941 writers like J. B. Priestley and Ritchie Calder[7] wrote about as if it had already begun, via blitzes and restaurants, seems less certain now. The Tories re-emerge with new assurance, while Labour hopes uncertainly. . . . What objective evidence can we now adduce about the probable emergent political pattern? Data accumulate, and certain tentative, limited answers can be attempted. . . .

The commonest single belief among politicians seems to be that at the next General Election, whatever Party or Group Winston Churchill heads will win (e.g. *Spectator*, Sept. 3rd; *Tribune*, October 22nd; Nicholas Davenport in *Evening Standard*, Nov. 3rd; Michael Foot in *Evening Standard*, Nov. 23rd). . . .

The rank and file of Labour M.P.s suspect another 1931 trap. Many evidently consider Churchill can carry the post-war election, and that they must work for victory only in a second post-war election. It can by no means be said that Labour is in very confident mood. . . . Some months ago I remarked, at a research meeting, that social surveys suggested a probable Labour victory, by a wide margin, at the next election, if Labour played for success now. Next day, a famous Labour journalist rang me up to query this 'amazing statement', and another wrote me asking for substantiation of 'so extravagent a claim'. . . .

Let us see the available evidence here. First, this question of Churchill. The common editorial and M.P. assumption of his post-war potency finds relatively little support in studies of public, let alone private, opinion. Supremely popular as he is today, this is

[7] A journalist noted for his radical ideas in the *Daily Herald*.

closely associated with the idea of Winston the War Leader, Bulldog of Battle, etc. Ordinary people widely assume that after the war he'll rest on his magnificent laurels. If he doesn't, many say they will withdraw support, believing him no man of peace, of domestic policy or human detail. This comes up over and again in diaries, letters, talk. . . .

On a broader front, there are a variety of M[ass]-O[bservation] polls on post-war voting intentions. These must be treated with great caution, the main point to bear in mind being that people tend always to give 'respectable', status quo, opinions to strangers (investigators). BIPO has also conducted several polls of interest in this connection, and they correspond closely with M-O's less statistical indices. In June and August 1943 they asked: 'If there was a General Election tomorrow, how would you vote?'. . . .

Would vote for	**June 1943**	**August 1943**
Conservative	25	23
Labour	38	39
Liberal	9	9
Communist	3	3
Common Wealth	2	1

We can now examine . . . evidence of the ballot box itself. . . . In the first six months of 1943 there were twelve contested by-elections, with total polls:

Official Government Candidates	111,842 votes
Other candidates	90,684 votes (54,412 for Common Wealth)

Thus 45 per cent of votes cast were against candidates in all cases receiving the full support and prestige of Winston Churchill, and lately of all the party leaders, in war-time when national unity remains a strong card . . . on stale register, favouring the old and better off, the least radical. . . .

What, then, does it all arrive at? Simply this: . . . Movements are often confused and even contradictory. Behind them lie a deep and growing disillusion with the efficacy of existing systems, doubt about the whole pattern of promise in our civilised life. . . . Yet I doubt if this cynicism is so deep-seated in relation at least to the small act of voting, as it seems. . . . And on the present form I have no doubt that the present Conservative Party, even if led by Mr Churchill, will not accomplish enough of itself to govern again, unless the alternatives commit suicide. This is about the first prediction I have ever dared make. It is offered, therefore, diffidently but definitely. My own *views* don't come into it. Tom Harrisson, 'Who'll win?', *Political Quarterly*, XV, 1944, pp. 21–32.

6
The 1945 general election

This final chapter focuses on Labour's landslide victory at the 1945 election. For many months before Germany was defeated in May 1945, it was clear that the Churchill coalition had served its purpose. Aside from deadlock over reconstruction, ministers were engaged in increasingly partisan exchanges, thus setting the scene for an election characterised by profound and often bitterly expressed disagreements. The extracts here trace the various stages of the campaign, from Churchill's opening 'gestapo' salvo through to the announcement of sweeping Labour gains in all parts of the country. As Clement Attlee went to Buckingham Palace to accept the King's invitation to form a government, perplexed politicians and commentators tried to fathom why 'the man who won the war' had so decisively 'lost the peace'.

6.1 The break-up of the coalition government

Soon after the death of Hitler, the parties began the process of manouevring for advantage in the events that led up to the formal ending of the coalition and the announcement of a general election.

Friday, May 18th The P.M. and Mrs C. set off for Chartwell and I went to Chequers to dine and await them. Meanwhile, after a Conservative meeting at No. 10 the P.M. has written to Attlee, Sinclair and Ernest Brown, saying that he hopes they will agree to preserve the Coalition till the end of the war with Japan but that he cannot agree to fixing a date for an election in the autumn since that would mean an attempt to carry on the Government in an atmosphere of faction and electioneering. Attlee came to see the P.M. at the Annexe and was favourably disposed to trying to persuade his party to continue at its Whitsun Blackpool conference. He has Ernest Bevin with him in this.

Monday, May 21st . . . Attlee rang up from his Blackpool conference and gave his reply to the P.M.'s letter which was negative. At once all was swept aside and electioneering became the only topic, while the P.M., Macmillan and Randolph all tried their hands at drafting a reply to Attlee. They think they have manoeuvred skilfully, by placing on the Labour Party the onus of refusing to continue and of preferring faction to unity at a time when great dangers still remain. I don't think the P.M. is quite happy about this, but for all the other Tory politicians the time has now passed 'when none were for the party and all were for the state'. The most assiduous intriguer and hard-working electioneer is Lord Beaverbrook.

Wednesday, May 23rd The P.M. went to the Palace at noon, as pre-arranged, and asked to resign. Then there was a pause, as the P.M. was anxious to emphasise to the public that the King has the right to decide for whom he shall send, and at 4.00 he returned to be invited to form a new, and a Conservative, Government. On the whole I think the people are on the P.M.'s side in this preliminary skirmish and it is generally supposed that many will vote for the Conservatives merely out of personal loyalty to W.S.C. Parliament will be dissolved in three weeks and the election will be on July 5th.

Colville, *Fringes of Power*: entries for 18–23 May 1945, pp. 600–2.

6.2 The 'caretaker' government

In the interim period between the break-up of the coalition and polling day, Churchill presided over a 'caretaker' administration; its composition pointed to the likely shape of the cabinet that would follow a Conservative election victory on 5 July.

As soon as victory began to look assured, the War Cabinet ceased to be a united or indeed an effective body. Disputes and disagreements began to paralyse action. Defeat knits together, victory opens the seams. . . . The Prime Minister tried hard to keep the Coalition together and brought all his unique powers of persuasion to bear. His efforts were in vain: our Labour colleagues had decided to leave. . . .

Winston set about forming a new Government. He sent for me late one afternoon, and I found him in bed. He began very tentatively by saying that the War Cabinet was a thing of the past, a new Cabinet of sixteen Ministers would be formed.

'You, Oliver, of course are assured a place, but what place? . . . It had occured to me to ask you what you would think of the Admiralty: if you liked it, you would still be one of the sixteen.'

I answered: 'I should like it above all else. A service department has always been my dearest wish'. . . . Winston, who thought that I should regard the Admiralty as demotion, was much moved by my answer.[1] Tears coursed down his cheeks. 'My dear First Lord', he said, wringing my hand, 'that's splendid: we shall still be together: I thought you would like it. All the arrangements should be completed by tomorrow. By the way, I shall now send Brendan to the Board of Trade.'

I was quite delighted, but when I told Wyndham Portal[2] in confidence what was toward, he was much shocked. 'You have been put down a grade, Oliver,' he said. 'Winston will run the war against Japan for Great Britain and you will only be a lieutenant or chief of staff. He will try to run the Admiralty over your head.'

Though I was a little disturbed by the remarks of this shrewd observer, I said that I was completely indifferent to matters of grade; that I was sick of figures and production, industrialists, trade union leaders, exports and imports, exchange crises . . . statistics and statisticians, and looked forward to drinking port with admirals in their cabins and going on deck with them to get a breath of fresh air in my lungs. And Admiralty House: what a home, and the Board Room with those jolly wind-swept faces around me and the wind-vane swinging above one's head, and those marble dolphins adorning the fireplace. I inhabited Admiralty House in my imagination all that afternoon and evening, and went to bed happy. I threw down a volume of statistics about trade and slept as a First Lord should.

About 10 a.m., the Prime Minister rang me up. A weary voice said:

[1] Oliver Lyttelton had been Minister of Production since early 1942.
[2] Viscount Portal, who served as Minister of Works and Planning 1942–44.

'I'm sorry, it has all had to be changed . . . you are back where you were as Minister of Production and President of the Board of Trade. I'm sorry.'

I recovered my book of statistics from the waste-paper basket and sadly set myself to study the figures.

The new Cabinet met. Looking around, I was interested to see how hardy is the political tradition of many families. . . . The Prime Minister was the son of a Chancellor of the Exchequer; Anthony Eden a descendant of a Governor-General and Viceroy of India, who later became First Lord of the Admiralty; Lord Salisbury the son of a distinguished Minister and grandson of a Prime Minister; Lord Rosebery and Dick Law were both sons of a Prime Minister; . . . 'Rab' Butler the son of one of the most distinguished Colonial Governors; Harold Macmillan was allied by marriage to the Cavendish family; . . . I was the son of a Secretary of State for the Colonies.

The whole atmosphere had changed overnight: tension had relaxed. No one amongst the sixteen, other than perhaps the Prime Minister and the Foreign Secretary, was particularly anxious to remain in office, although the majority of us thought that we should be condemned to a further four years.

Oliver Lyttelton, *The Memoirs of Lord Chandos*, London, 1962, pp. 322–5.

6.3 Churchill's 'Gestapo' speech

The Prime Minister opened the election campaign with an infamous radio broadcast. His broadside against the menace of socialism dismayed many of his own supporters, and set the tone for the bitter exchanges that were to follow.

Socialism is, in its essence, an attack not only upon British enterprise, but upon the right of the ordinary man or woman to breathe freely without a harsh, clumsy, tyrannical hand clapped across their mouths. . . .

No Socialist system can be estalished without a political police. Many of those who are advocating Socialism or voting Socialist will be horrified at this idea. That is because they are short-sighted . . . they do not see where their theories are leading them.

No Socialist Government . . . could allow free, sharp, or violently worded expressions of public discontent. They would have to fall back on some form of Gestapo. . . . And this would nip opinion in the bud; it would stop criticism as it reared its head, and it would gather all the power to the supreme party and the party leaders, rising like stately pinnacles above their vast bureaucracies of Civil Servants, no longer servants and no longer civil. And where would the common people be, once this mighty organism had got them in its grip?

Party Political Broadcast by Mr Churchill, BBC Radio, 4 June 1945.

6.4 Reaction to Churchill's speech

Churchill's doctor noted in his diary how the Prime Minister had hit the wrong note in his 'Gestapo' speech, and had allowed Attlee to take the initiative in the early part of the campaign.

June 4 I am staying at Professor Wynn's house in Birmingham, where I have come to examine students, and we were checking the marks in the papers when Wynn proposed that we should break off to listen to the Prime Minister's broadcast. 'It's the kick-off in the election campaign.'

When it was done I glanced round the room. It was plain that it had not gone down with anybody. Cloake thought it was all negative, just abuse of the Socialists; Wynn felt that it was out of tune with the forces that are trying to plan a better world: his daughter considered it 'cheap'. No one agreed with the line that Winston had taken. He scoffs at 'those foolish people' who want to rebuild the world, but beneath this bluster he is, I believe, less certain about things. He has a feeling that he is back in the thirties, alone in the world, speaking a foreign tongue. . . .

June 5 Attlee, the 'poor Clem' of the war years, did his piece tonight, and did it well.[3] Perhaps his years in Bermondsey have brought home to him that politics are more than a game. At any rate, as I listened, it became plain that one ounce of Gladstone's moral fervour was worth a ton of skilled invective. And this in spite of the

[3] Each of the parties was allocated a series of radio election broadcasts; Attlee's first effort was generally considered to be a dignified and effective response to Churchill's invective.

handicap of Attlee's delivery. It is clear that the P.M. is on the wrong tack; Max and Brendan are his advisers, and he will not learn from anyone else. For the first time the thought went through my head that he may lose the election.

Lord Moran, *Winston Churchill: The Struggle for Survival 1940–1965*, London, 1966, pp. 275–6.

6.5 'Dreamland'

The cartoonist David Low was one amongst many who mocked Churchill's 'Gestapo' claims; here the Prime Minister is seen flanked by Bracken and Beaverbrook, who were rumoured (incorrectly) to have written the notorious radio broadcast.

David Low, Dreamland, *Evening Standard*, 7 June 1945.

6.6 The early phase of the campaign in the constituencies

Many voters were rather bewildered by the bitterness of the opening exchanges. This came across in a report by Mass-Observation, which recorded both general impressions in London and particular responses in the constituency of Fulham.

In mid-June, among Londoners asked how they felt, about the peace now, only one in seven said they were happy or elated. A third said they felt no different from during the war; a quarter felt worried (half for international reasons); 15% felt depressed; and several simply said that there ought not to be an election yet.

Into this atmosphere of war weariness, disappointment and bewilderment came the announcement of the General Election. It might have been expected that such an announcement would act as a tonic on the drooping populace, inspiring them with new hope and excitement, and giving them the feeling that at last things were going to be coped with. And, had the campaign been conducted in a different manner this might well have been the public reaction. But as it was, the election campaign was ushered in by violent and abusive denunciations of each party by the other, filling the press and radio for a number of days, all of them deploring the fact that there should be an election at all, and blaming the other side for having forced it upon the country. It it difficult to conceive of an electioneering technique better calculated to lower the morale of an already dispirited electorate. . . .

The election campaign may be said to have begun with the speech Mr Churchill broadcast to the nation on the evening of June 4th. It would be difficult to exaggerate the disappointment and genuine distress aroused by this speech: indeed, it would hardly be too much to say that it was in large measure this speech that set the whole tone of the election, and made inevitable the spirit of disillusion and cynicism with which the country as a whole greeted the opening of the campaign. . . .

[Our] investigator records her own impressions of the campaign in Fulham, thus:

. . . 'During the first week of the election campaign in E[ast] Fulham people showed little interest in the election. . . . Then appeared Churchill's letter in the press, saying that Labour had more or less forced this election. Labour retaliated by saying that Churchill and his party hoped to profit by a snap election. And the daily press, instead of clarifying matters, only confused the issues by resorting to heavy type and sensational headlines, and bewildering people with conflicting viewpoints. . . .

Churchill's speech – the Gestapo-Savings scare – comes in for a good deal of criticism from all parties, and is generally felt for a man of Churchill's prestige to be a very poor effort, and a cheapening electioneering speech. . . .

The cross-section interviewed this week weighs heavily in the direction of Labour, but it is as yet too soon to make election predictions, since a large proportion of contacts haven't yet made up their minds, and are likely to be swayed by (a) personalities, (b) phoney election stunts. Both are possible.'

Mass-Observation, Typescript Report No. 2268, 'The General Election June–July 1945', October 1945, pp. 4, 10 and 81–4.

6.7 The Conservative manifesto

After the acrimony of the first week, the campaign settled down gradually with a greater focus on policy issues, as raised by the respective party manifestos. Conservative determination to exploit the Prime Minister's popularity was reflected in the title of 'Mr Churchill's Declaration'.

I had hoped to preserve the Coalition Government, comprising all Parties in the State, until the end of the Japanese War, but owing to the unwillingness of the Socialist and Sinclair Liberal parties to agree to my proposal, a General Election became inevitable, and I have formed a new National Government, consisting of the best men in all parties who were willing to serve and some who are members of no party at all. . . .

We seek the good of the whole nation, not that of one section or one faction. We believe in the living unity of the British people, which transcends class or party differences. It was this living unity which enabled us to stand like a rock against Germany when she overran Europe. Upon our power to retain unity, the future of this country and of the whole world largely depends.

Britain is still at war, and must not turn aside from the vast further efforts still needed to bring Japan to the same end as Germany. Even when all foreign enemies are utterly defeated, that will not be the end of our task. It will be the beginning of our further opportunity – the opportunity which we snatched out of the jaws of disaster in 1940 – to save the world from tyranny and to play our part in its wise, helpful guidance. . . .

The settlement of Europe and the prosecution of the war against Japan depend on decisions of the utmost gravity, which can only be taken by resolute and experienced men. Our alliance with Soviet Russia and our intimate friendship with the U.S.A. can be maintained only if we show that our candour is matched by our strength. . . .

We shall base the whole of our international policy on a recognition that in world affairs the Mother Country must act in the closest possible concert with all other parts of the British Commonwealth and Empire. We shall never forget their love and steadfastness when we stood alone against the German Terror. We, too, have done our best for them. . . .

More than two years ago I made a broadcast to the nation in which I sketched a four-years' plan which would cover five or six large measures of a practical character, which must all have been the subject of prolonged, careful and energetic preparation beforehand, and which fitted together into a general scheme. This plan has now been shaped, and we present it to the country for their approval. . . .

The Government accepts as one of its primary aims and responsibilites the maintenance of a high and stable level of employment. Unless there is steady and ample work, there will not be the happiness, the confidence or the material resources in the country on which we can all build together the kind of Britain that we want to see.

To find plenty of work with individual liberty to choose one's job, free enterprise must be given the chance and the encouragement to plan ahead. Confidence in sound government – mutual co-operation between industry and the State, rather than control by the State, and lightening the burdens of excessive taxation – these are the first essentials. . . .

We should examine the conditions and the vital needs of every industry on its merits. We believe in variety, not in standardised and identical structure, still less in bureaucratic torpor. We will not allow drastic changes of ownership to be forced upon industry with no evidence except a political theory, and with no practical regard to the results they will bring. To us the tests will always be – what will conduce most to efficiency, and what will render the greatest service to the community. This is the policy we shall apply, whether it be for coal, cotton or the heavy industries. . . .

On a basis of high employment, initiative and hard work on the part of everyone, we can achieve our great Four Years' programme. It is well worth achieving.

The Conservative Party, *Mr. Churchill's Declaration of Policy to the Electors*, 1945.

6.8 **Labour's manifesto**

The Labour party's manifesto was very different in tone and emphasis: placing domestic before international affairs and highlighting the need for collectivist solutions to the problems of reconstruction.

Britain's coming election will be the greatest test in our history of the judgement and common sense of our people. . . .

The problems and pressures of the post-war world threaten our security and progress as surely as – though less dramatically than – the Germans threatened them in 1940. We need the spirit of Dunkirk and of the Blitz sustained over a period of years.

The Labour Party's programme is a practical expression of that spirit applied to the tasks of peace. It calls for hard work, energy and sound sense.

We must prevent another war, and that means that we must have such an international organisation as will give all nations real security against future aggression. But Britain can only play her full part in such an international plan if our spirit as shown in our handling of home affairs is firm, wise and determined. This statement of policy, therefore, begins at home. . . .

The nation needs a tremendous overhaul, a great programme of modernisation of its homes, its factories and machinery, its schools, its social services.

All parties say so – the Labour Party means it. For the Labour Party is prepared to achieve it by drastic policies of replanning and by keeping a firm constructive hand on our whole productive machinery; the Labour Party will put the community first and the sectional interests of private business after. . . .

What will the Labour Party do?

First, the whole of the national resources, in land, material and labour must be fully employed. Production must be raised to the highest level and related to purchasing power. . . . It is doubtful whether we have ever, except in war, used the whole of our productive capacity. This must be corrected because, upon our ability to produce and organise a fair and generous distribution of the product, the standard of living of our people depends.

Secondly, a high and constant purchasing power can be maintained through good wages, social services and insurance, and taxation which bears less heavily on the lower-income groups. But everybody knows that money and savings lose their value if prices rise, so rents and the prices of necessities of life will be controlled.

Thirdly, planned investment in essential industries and on houses, schools, hospitals and civic centres will occupy a large field of capital expenditure. A National Investment Board will determine social priorities and promote better timing in private investment. . . . The location of new factories will be suitably controlled, and where necessary the Government will itself build factories. There must be no depressed areas in the New Britain. . . .

Each industry must have applied to it the test of national service. If it serves the nation, well and good; if it is inefficient and falls down on the job, the nation must see that things are put right.

These propositions seem indisputable, but for years before the war anti-Labour Governments set them aside, so that British industry over a large field fell into a state of depression, muddle and decay. Millions of working and middle-class people went through the horrors of unemployment and insecurity. It is not enough to sympathise with these victims: we must develop an acute feeling of national shame – and act.

The Labour Party is a Socialist Party, and proud of it. Its ultimate purpose at home is the establishment of the Socialist Commonwealth of Great Britain – free, democratic, efficient, progressive, public-spirited, its material resources organised in the service of the British people.

The Labour Party, *Let us Face the Future: A Declaration of Labour Policy for the Consideration of the Nation*, 1945.

6.9 The mid-way point in the campaign

In winding up his wartime diary, the Prime Minister's personal secretary reflected both on events abroad and the drift of the election at home.

Over all Europe hangs the cloud of insufficient supplies, disjointed distribution, lack of coal and a superfluity of destitute and displaced persons. The situation is no easier, nor are the prospects apparently brighter, than before the first shot was fired.

At home the first intoxication of victory is passing. The parties are creating bitterness, largely artificial, in their vote-catching hysteria. Brendan and the Beaver are firing vast salvos which mostly, I think, miss their mark. Labour propaganda is a great deal better and is launched on a rising market. Without Winston's personal prestige the Tories would not have a chance. Even with him I am not sanguine of their prospects, though most of their leaders are confident of a good majority. I think the service vote will be Left and the housing shortage has left many people disgruntled. The main Consrevative advantage is the prevailing good humour of the people and the accepted point that Attlee would be a sorry successor to Winston at the meeting of the Big Three and in the counsels of the Nations.

Colville, *Fringes of Power*: entry for 18 June 1945, p. 607.

6.10 The Laski affair

Labour did not have things all its own way in the final stages of the campaign. For several days newspapers ran scare stories about how Labour was manipulated by extra-parliamentary forces: this followed an ill-timed comment by Professor Harold Laski, Chairman of Labour's NEC, that Attlee should go with the Prime Minister to the peace conference at Potsdam only as an observer.

The Laski affair was most irritating. I don't think it will have turned over very many votes and I only once – at Grimsby – got a question on it in all my meetings, but it was worked up into a mild scare which will have brought out a certain number of old women who otherwise would not have voted. Laski should not have intervened, in the first instance, on the invitation to Attlee to go to Berlin. He was not in touch with the Parliamentary leaders or would have known that they had been consulted and agreed; nor could there have been any question of us being 'bound' by decisions reached in Berlin, now that we are no longer in the Government; nor, on the other hand, is it very likely that we should wish to line up against anything agreed to, not only by Churchill, but by Stalin and Truman;[4] nor should professors use words loosely – in this case the word 'observer' which, in relation to conferences, always means a dumb person at the conference table, obviously an impossible position. But this silly little intervention gave the Tories just what they had lacked till then. A plausible new bogy. It is a pity his name was Laski, and not Smith, and that he was not a Member of Parliament. The question of the relationship of the National Executive to the Parliamentary leaders is, in fact, slightly delicate, though there is nothing new about it. It is not a thing the public discussion of which brings any gain to us. A further fuss, as to whether the little fool said that in any circumstances we should 'use violence' – I always find it rather comic that this contingency should be discussed by this puny, short-sighted, weak-hearted, rabbinical-looking little chap! – has been stopped for the moment by the issue of writs, a very sensible move. But I have a sort of suspicion that here too he said something he should not.

Pimlott (ed.), *Political Diary of Hugh Dalton*: entry for July 1945, p. 357.

6.11 **On the campaign trail**

The Labour party generally seemed in confident mood, as this sketch by one of its young candidates shows. Like many, Aidan Crawley had served in the forces (being a prisoner of war) and

[4] President Harry Truman, representing the United States after the death of Roosevelt.

was only adopted as a candidate shortly before the election.

Desmond Donnelly of the Commonwealth Party had already telephoned me to say that although he had been keeping warm my candidature in north Buckinghamshire (a fact of which I was ignorant) he had already withdrawn as the local Labour Party was solidly behind me. To fight the election I had persuaded two former camp inmates to come and help me: Robert Kee and Philip Moore . . ., both ten years younger than I and keen Labour supporters. We went down to Buckingham to find somewhere to live. I rented for a month Lone Tree Cottage, about two miles outside the town, belonging to a Mrs Lynes. It was ideal, no electric light or mains water but very cheap, with three bedrooms and a hand pump in the garden at which we would wash and shave. After being away so long we all had the zeal of missionaries, canvassed every village in the constituency, held meetings in the evenings, usually in the open air because the weather was fine, visited Working Men's Clubs, factories, the railway wagon works in Wolverton and Co-operative stores wherever they existed. Teams of enthusiastic local supporters accompanied us. . . .

Our opponents did not take the onslaught lying down. Their candidate, Lionel Berry, son of Lord Kemsley, was respectable but staid; some of his supporters less so. One of our posters was a larger-than-life picture of myself wearing a Royal Air Force cap. Lionel's cousin, Pamela Berry, who lived in the neighbouring constituency, went round painting my lips red wherever she could reach them. . . .

The climax of the campaign was the eve of poll meeting in the Town Hall of Buckingham. More than a thousand people had crammed into the hall, many of them standing. In my speech I had just said that I thought it was time that cottages in Buckinghamshire were supplied with mains water and electricity, implying that a Labour Government would see that they got it, when a very large old lady whom I recognized as my landlady, Mrs Lynes, got up at the back of the hall and said that she owned many cottages in the constituency and could assure Mr Crawley that all of them were equipped with electric light and mains water. I said quite gently, 'Mrs Lynes, I think you must have forgotten that at the moment I am living in Lone Tree Cottage, which belongs to you. I must tell the audience that it has no water, except for a hand-pump in the garden . . ., and no electricity.' The whole audience roared with laughter and Mrs Lynes left the meeting very angry. When Robert, Philip and I got home later that night, we found all our bedding, sheets, blankets, towels and pillow cases festooning the bushes and trees in the garden. Mrs Lynes had been in and thrown them all out of the windows.[5]

Aidan Crawley, *Leap Before You Look*, London, 1988, pp. 207–9.

6.12 Summing up the campaign

Some political commentators believed that the campaign had not been well handled by either of the main parties.

At last the long election campaign is over, and the relief of the man in the street will be almost as great as it was when the military campaign in Europe, also over-lengthy, finally drew to a close. . . .

After ten years of world-shaking events, after the transition from one era to another, after the emergence of a whole array of new problems – after all this a thoughtful, well-reasoned, factual confrontation of competing policies might legitimately have been expected. Instead, not only has there been an almost complete failure to clarify issues, but there has been a determination to evade them and ride off on irrelevancies. In the constituencies, a large part of the blame for this must unquestionably be put upon the Labour and Communist parties. It is becoming almost a rule now, especially in urban areas, that Labour meetings are orderly, but that Labour hecklers do their best to prevent free speech at Conservative, and often at Liberal meetings. . . .

But on the national stage, in the newspapers and on the wireless, the roles have been reversed. Here the Labour Party has conducted its campaign with great dignity and good feeling, while the Conservatives have resorted to stunts, red herrings and unfair practices to an extent that has disgusted many of their friends and followers – and, if the truth could be told, most of their leaders outside the charmed circle. The constructive moderation of Mr Eden, Mr Butler and Sir John Anderson has, with the Prime Minister's active help,

[5] Crawley won the contest with a majority of 3,845.

been overriden by the circus. The Beaverbrook press has promised everything from speedier demobilisation to economic miracles as a result of a Tory victory and these papers have also seemed to be the whippers-in for the whole pack in the Laski affair. This has been grotesquely inflated. . . .

For any friend of democracy, it is a very shocking thing to have to record, but Mr Churchill's harping on the Laski theme in the last few days before the poll was nothing but an unworthy stunt, as insulting to the intelligence of the electorate as it was to the patriotism of the Labour leaders. . . .

In this election . . . the radio speeches have probably very greatly aided the elector in his perplexity, since they were so evenly balanced in their merits and defects. When all is said and done, they have not encouraged very many hopes that either of the major parties would confront the enormous and novel tasks of the next few years with the energy that the predicament of the country requires. Such things as foreign and imperial policy, the maintenance of high and stable employment, the drastic overhaul of British industrial methods, the carrying of the enormous burden of external indebtedness, the preservation of industrial peace and social unity – all these things require heavy effort and great skill. . . . On many of them the Labour Party is ready to proclaim the need for drastic action, but the Tories, if only they could be led to see what needs to be done, would be most competent to do it. And as between a party which will but cannot and one which could but will not, it is hard to choose.

The Economist, 7 July 1945.

6.13 **Predicting the outcome**

After the polls had closed, Labour leaders found it difficult to believe that Churchill could be beaten, notwithstanding the blunder of his Gestapo speech and anecdotal evidence that suggested otherwise.

The election was very long drawn out. It went on for nearly six weeks. . . . I was totally tired, by the end of it, of hearing myself repeat the same old arguments and phrases night by night. I spoke for thirty-two candidates other than myself. . . . In a number of constituencies, where it would be close anyhow, I thought the personality of our candidate would just make the difference. On the other hand, but for the personality of the P.M., I thought we should trample the Tories underfoot and get a large majority. In fact, I much over-estimated the P.M.'s personal influence on votes. . . .

As the war in Europe drew towards the end, the P.M., I heard, said to Air Chief Marshal Harris: 'I suppose that, when the election comes, I can count on the votes of most of the men in the Air Force?' 'No, sir,' replied Harris, 'eighty per cent of them will vote Labour.' 'Well at least that will give me 20 per cent', said the P.M., sharply taken aback. 'No, sir, the other 20 per cent won't vote at all'. . . .

We polled on July 5th. Then I went away to West Leaze for three weeks, returning on July 25th for the count. Hopes had been rising since the poll, but I still couldn't persuade myself that we could have won more than 280 seats. Probably, therefore, there would be either a small Tory majority or a deadlock.

Hugh Dalton, *The Fateful Years: Memoirs 1931–1945*, London, 1957, pp. 463–6.

6.14 The election results announced

The full results were not announced until 26 July in order to allow service votes to arrive from different parts of the world. Some Conservative MPs like Amery took the result stoically, even though he and many of his colleagues in Birmingham were defeated.

Landslide. To the count at 9.00 and very soon saw that Shurmer would be in by thousands. . . . well before 11.00 the result was announced, Shurmer 14,085, myself 8,431, a majority of 5,634. . . . All the other Birmingham seats have gone except Paddy Hannon,[6] Handsworth and Edgbaston. As the morning wore on the news came in of the same landslide everywhere. It looks as if Conservatives could not now be returned more than about 220 strong. Most of the present Ministers have gone except Winston himself, the two Olivers [Lyttelton and Stanley], Anthony [Eden] and Rob Hudson.

Personally, I cannot help feeling amused and indeed cheered. All

[6] Sir Patrick Hannon, Conservative MP for Birmingham Moseley.

this opens a new chapter in one's life and that always has a rejuvenating effect. So far as the country is concerned it is far better that the Socialists should come in now harnessed between the shafts of the war machine and the international situation, not to speak of facing all domestic problems like housing, demobilisation, coal, etc. This is far better than that a weak and weary Conservative administration should be turned out three years hence and succeeded by 15 years of Socialist government. As it is there is at any rate some hope of the Conservative Party reforming itself, though unless it recovers an ideal and a method it will never again enthuse the country or get in other than as a mere stop gap between two Socialist administrations. . . . For Winston the result is I think a godsend. Instead of petering out amid all the worries of a declining government he goes out at the height of his fame and can sit down and write what no-one else can, the history of these great years.

Barnes and Nicholson (eds), *Amery Diary*: entry for 26 July 1945, pp. 1048–9.

6.15 Conservative reaction to defeat

Not all Conservatives were as philosophical as Amery about the outcome. A more typical response came from the MP for Newcastle North, Cuthbert Headlam.

We got to Newcastle about 11 o'clock this morning and our result was declared at 12.30. The figures were self 17381: Shackleton 10228: McKeag 5812: Ridsdaly 904. It was a great relief – and a famous victory in this truly catastrophic election – never was such a crushing disaster – the 3 other Newcastle seats have gone and except for a victory at Berwick where Beveridge was turned out,[7] we have only one other seat in the whole Northern Area – Penrith & Cockermouth. It is the same story all over the country. Labour has a clear majority of 150 or thereabout over 'the rest' – Winston has resigned and little Mr Attlee reigns instead – it is a sorry business and one feels ashamed of one's countrymen. But there it is, this is democracy – the people wanted a change, and no longer being afraid,

[7] Beveridge had won a by-election at Berwick, standing as a Liberal, in October 1944.

voted Labour. The Left Wing propaganda has had its affect and it would seem that the vast majority of the new generation has gone Socialist for the time being. What a H[ouse] of C[ommons] it is going to be – filled with young, half-baked, young men mainly from the R.A.F. so far as I can make out.

Ball (ed.), *Headlam diary*, 26 July 1945.

6.16 Labour reaction to victory

The sense of surprise and elation on the Labour side was captured by Chuter Ede, MP for South Shields, who having started political life as a Liberal compared the result with the Liberal landslide of 1906.

Thursday 26 July I did not wake up until 8 a.m. & just managed to get to the Town Hall by nine o'clock. Gompertz[8] & all his checkers were there. All were in high spirits & certain that they had won. The Mayor came over to me and said he had thought that our majority would be over 1500 but he thought, after the papers he had seen yesterday that we should do much better than that. . . . The Mayor then went into the main room where he announced the final figures as:–

Ede 22,410
Parry 15,296
Giving a Labour Majority of 7,114. . . .

[Then] at 12 noon came the staggering announcement: 'The Government hold 24 seats; the Opposition 100. . . . ' Bracken, Amery, Grigg, Sandys, Lloyd, Macmillan, Somervell & Hore-Belisha[9] were all stated to be out. . . . I began to wonder if I should wake up to find it all a dream. The 3 p.m. announcement opened with a statement that Labour now with 364 seats had a clear majority over all others. . . . All Tyneside had voted Socialist. All the Durham County seats had been held & we appeared to have won all the Durham Boroughs. . . . In Greater London there were 32 Labour gains. Manchester returned only one Tory; Birmingham has 3 Tories and 10 Lab. . . .

[8] Ede's agent in the South Shields constituency.
[9] All ministers in the caretaker government.

This is as great as 1906. I warned Butler more than once that one day the nation, voting on one day, would swing violently left. I had expected it to be at the election following this but the hatred of the Tories has been so great that they have been swept out of office by a tidal wave. This is one of the unique occasions in British history – a Red Letter day in the best sense of that term. . . . Churchill had gone to Buckingham Palace, where he had resigned. Attlee had been summoned and had accepted the King's invitation to form a Govt. . . .

Saturday 28 July As I had often foretold, the country desiring to give power to the Left had followed the precedent of 1906 when it installed the steady, faithful but uninspiring Campbell-Bannerman. Attlee is no firework but the country found that Churchill had produced the appropriate background for our Party's set piece. Attlee's speech was typical.[10] Without a trace of emotion he alluded to the tremendous nature of our victory. . . . We were not going to postpone bringing in our measures. This session we should submit our programme. This determination moved the gathering to great enthusiasm. . . . The new Party is a great change from the old. It teems with bright, vivacious servicemen. The superannuated Trade Union official seems hardly to be noticeable in the ranks.

Jefferys (ed.), *Chuter Ede Diary*: entries for 26 and 28 July 1945, pp. 226–9.

6.17 Labour's perspective on the 1945 result: never again

How did Labour politicians see their victory, looking back with the benefit of hindsight? Ede's emphasis on the 'never again' mentality of 1945 was also evident in later accounts, such as the autobiography of Jim Callaghan.

I made many speeches in favour of our proposals for a universal Health Service and comprehensive social security, and campaigned for a vigorous prosecution of the war against Japan. But most of the questions were about demobilisation from the Forces or about housing shortages. In my innocence and in good faith I promised rapid action on both, and during the campaign my main slogan

[10] At a party meeting in London hastily convened to celebrate victory.

became, 'We built the Spitfires. Now we can build the houses'. The result was a stunning victory. Our majority in Cardiff was bigger than even we had dreamed possible, and I had the experience of being carried shoulder-high from the City Hall in triumph through a host of our supporters.

Labour won all three Cardiff seats from the Conservatives. George Thomas, who had been adopted for Cardiff Central, received the same exuberant treatment and together we were borne precariously away.

Men and women twice our age who had hoped all their lives to see this day were overcome with emotion, and amid the cheering I saw tears of joy. They were thinking that never again would our people return to the unemployment of the 1930s. Never again would sons and daughters leave their homes so that their parents could avoid the means test. No longer would men and women be crushed by blind economic forces. Instead, we would use economics to serve the people's needs. Hospital treatment, decent houses to live in, and pensions in old age would banish want. Nothing was impossible. We were unconquerable.

James Callaghan, *Time and Chance*, London, 1987, pp. 63–4.

6.18 A 'Chamberlainite' perspective on the 1945 election

In rationalising the outcome from their own perspective, Conservatives often revived the old party divisions of 1938–40. As a one-time supporter of Chamberlain, Rab Butler was criticial of Churchill's handling of the election.

Like Churchill himself, but unlike most of his influential colleagues, I was very strongly in favour of maintaining an all-party National Government. . . . This seemed best in the national interest; in the party's interest it seemed imperative. Our organisation up and down the country was in a parlous condition, much harder hit than that of our opponents by the absence of agents and organizers on war service. Our policy, on which David Maxwell Fyfe[11] and I had been working sporadically since 1941 at the head of the Post-War Problems Committee, was as yet insufficiently, if at all, disseminated in

[11] Conservative MP and Solicitor-General 1942–45.

the constituencies. At a meeting of the principal Conservative members of the Coalition, which was presided over by Churchill in the Cabinet room, I therefore argued that the Conservatives were not ready for an election in 1945 and that, if one were held, the result would be disastrous. Beaverbrook came up to me afterwards and said, 'Young man, if you speak to the Prime Minister like that, you will not be offered a job in the next Conservative government.' I replied, 'That doesn't really affect me; for if we have an early election, there is not going to be a Conservative government.'

Churchill bore me no grudge for the warning. He was himself in great perplexity, even agony, of mind – 'deeply distressed', in his own words, 'at the prospect of sinking from a national to a party leader'. Unfortunately, the great man was seldom able to do things by halves, and the sinking was therefore altogether deeper than it needed to be. His first election broadcast, with its rollicking polemic against Socialism which, he said, could not be established without a 'Gestapo', was by common consent a strategic blunder. . . .

The Churchill-Attlee exchange was a pivotal event in the history of the election and set its tone; but it did not, I believe, affect the final verdict. It was sad that the work done by the Post-War Problems Committee played so little part in the formulation of our Conservative campaign, and that the conduct of the election swept away much of the idealism which we wanted to instil and which emerged only in the 1945–51 period in opposition. It would have been better if affirmation of post-war policies had not taken a poor third place to the concentrated exploitation of Churchill's personality and a negative attack on the Labour Party. But the election would probably have been lost in any case. . . . I was – to an extent of which at the time I was unaware – on a completely different wave-length from millions of voters who . . . wanted, or at least thought they wanted, a great deal turned upside down.

Butler, *Art of the Possible*, pp. 126–9.

6.19 A 'Churchillite' perspective on the 1945 election

In contrast to Butler, Harold Macmillan – one of those who worked to bring down Chamberlain in 1940 – was much more sympathetic towards Churchill, and had no doubt who was primarily responsible for defeat in 1945.

As soon as electioneering began in earnest I knew what the result would would be. . . . Many people believed that Churchill's first speech on the wireless was a turning point to our disadvantage. It was certainly unbalanced and ill-advised . . . [and] at the time it shocked as well as angered ordinary folk. I do not believe, however, that this incident was in any way decisive. The election in my view, was lost before it started.

Churchill was buoyed up by the enthusastic reception which he had received in his 1000-mile electoral tour. Vast crowds, who had hardly seen in him person since the beginning of the war and only heard his voice through those famous broadcasts, by which they had been sustained in times of disaster and inspired at moments of success, turned out in flocks to see and applaud him. They wished to thank him for what he had done for them; and in that all were sincere. But this did not mean that they wished to entrust him and his Tory colleagues with the conduct of their lives in the years that were to follow. They had been persuaded, civilians and Servicemen alike, during the last years of the war, that immediately the struggle was over there would follow a kind of automatic Utopia. The British people would move with hardly an effort into a Socialist or semi-Socialist State under their own leaders, which would bring about unexampled prosperity in a world of universal peace. Nor had they forgotten or been allowed to forget the years before the war. Pamphlets and books attacking the 'guilty men of Munich' were published and circulated in vast numbers. It was not Churchill who lost the 1945 election; it was the ghost of Neville Chamberlain.

Harold Macmillan, *Tides of Fortune 1945–1955*, London, 1979, pp. 31–2.

Guide to further reading

General

Wartime politics receive broad treatment in a variety of textbooks on modern Britain, such as Kenneth Morgan's excellent study *The People's Peace. British History 1945–1989*, Oxford 1990. More specialised secondary works include Henry Pelling, *Britain and the Second World War*, London, 1970; Paul Addison, *The Road to 1945, British Politics and the Second World War*, London, 1975; J. M. Lee, *The Churchill Coalition 1940–45*, London, 1980; Kevin Jefferys, *The Churchill Coalition and Wartime Politics 1940–1945*, Manchester, 1991; Stephen Brooke, *Labour's War. The Labour Party during the Second World War*, Oxford 1992; and Brian Brivati and Harriet Jones (eds), *What Difference did the War Make?*, Leicester, 1993.

Students seeking published primary sources might begin with two volumes in the 'Cambridge Topics in History' series: Paul Adelman, *British Politics in the 1930s and 1940s*, Cambridge, 1987; and Jocelyn Hunt and Sheila Watson, *Britain and the two World Wars*, Cambridge, 1990.

The role of the Labour party can be followed at the level of primary sources in Ben Pimlott (ed.), *The Second World War Diary of Hugh Dalton 1940–1945*, London, 1986; and Kevin Jefferys (ed.), *Labour and the Wartime Coalition: from the Diary of James Chuter Ede 1941–45*, London, 1987. On the Conservative side, see Robert Rhodes James (ed.), *Chips. The Diaries of Sir Henry Channon*, London, 1967; and Stuart Ball (ed.), *Parliament and Politics in the age of Churchill and Attlee: The Headlam Diaries 1935–1951*, London, forthcoming.

On Churchill as war leader, two important works containing primary source material are Lord Moran, *Winston Churchill. The Struggle for Survival*, London, 1966; and John Colville, *The Fringes of Power: Downing Street Diaries 1939–1955*, London, 1985. Churchill, of course, published his own six-volume history entitled *The Second World War* (individual volumes of which are cited in the chapters above), though this concentrates mainly on military and diplomatic rather than political developments.

There are numerous biographies of leading politicians that also provide coverage of the war years, e.g. B. Donoughue and G. W. Jones, *Herbert Morrison: Portrait of a Politician*, London, 1973; Martin Gilbert, *Winston S. Churchill*, Vol. VI, *Finest Hour 1939–41*, London, 1983 and Vol. VII, *Road to Victory 1941–45*, London, 1986; Kenneth Harris, *Attlee*, London, 1982; Ben Pimlott, *Hugh Dalton*, 1985; Keith Robbins, *Churchill*, London, 1992.

Visual evidence such as photographs can be found in several general histories of the period, such as Peter Lewis, *A People's War*, London, 1986. The famous cartoons of David Low are collected together in *Years of Wrath: a Cartoon History 1932–45*, London, 1986 edn.

The phoney war and the downfall of Neville Chamberlain

The early months of the war are best examined further through a series of journal articles: Jorgen Rasmussen, 'Party discipline in war-time: the downfall of the Chamberlain government', *Journal of Politics*, 32, 1970; D. M. Roberts, 'Clement Davies and the fall of Neville Chamberlain, 1939–40', *Welsh History Review*, 8, 1976; and Kevin Jefferys, 'May 1940: the downfall of Neville Chamberlain', *Parliamentary History*, 10, 2, 1991.

In addition to the diaries mentioned above, there are many contrasting examples of contemporary opinion during the phoney war. The pro-Chamberlainite recollections of Lord Home, *The Way the Wind Blows*, London, 1976, for instance, might be set against the anti-government views recorded in John Barnes and David Nicholson (eds), *The Empire at Bay: the Leo Amery Diaries 1929–1945*, London, 1988.

Churchill and Britain's 'finest hour'

Three recent studies which attempt to get behind some of the myths of Britain's 'finest hour' are Clive Ponting, *1940*, London, 1991; Angus Calder, *The Myth of the Blitz*, London, 1991; and Robert Blake and William Roger Louis (eds), *Churchill*, Oxford, 1993.

Three shorter pieces also shed light on aspects of high politics in 1940: Paul Addison, 'Lloyd George and compromise peace in the Second World War', in A. J. P. Taylor (ed), *Lloyd George: Twelve Essays*, London, 1971; David Dilks, 'The twilight war and the fall of France: Chamberlain and Churchill in 1940', in David Dilks (ed.), *Retreat from Power*, Vol. II, *After 1939*, London, 1981; and David Reynolds, 'Churchill and the British "decision" to fight on in 1940: right policy, wrong reasons', in R. Langhorne (ed.), *Diplomacy and Intelligence during the Second World War*, Cambridge, 1985.

The war and the war economy

Debate about the performance of Britain's war economy has been stimulated by Corelli Barnett's controversial work *The Audit of War: the Illusion and Reality of Britain as a Great Nation*, London, 1986. For critiques of Barnett's approach, see Paul Addison, 'The road from 1945', in Peter Hennessy and Anthony Seldon (eds), *Ruling Performance*, Oxford, 1987; and Jose Harris, 'Enterprise and the Welfare State: a Comparative Perspective', in Terry Gourvish and Alan O'Day (eds), *Britain since 1945*, Basingstoke and London, 1991.

Different aspects of the war economy are also highlighted in Alan Bullock, *The Life and Times of Ernest Bevin*, Vol. II, *Minister of Labour 1940–1945*, London, 1967; Alan Booth, 'The "Keynesian Revolution" in economic policy-making', *Economic History Review*, 36, 1, 1983; and Keith Middlemas, *Power, Competition and the State*, Vol. I, *Britian in Search of Balance, 1940–1961*, London, 1986. A useful overview for students is provided by Alan Milward, *The Economic Effects of the Two World Wars on Britain*, London, 1984.

On the threat to Churchill's authority as Prime Minister during late 1941–42, see G. M. Thomson, *Vote of Censure*, London, 1968; and David Day, *Menzies and Churchill at War*, Australia (Angus and Robertson), 1986.

The Beveridge Report and reconstruction

Several works by Jose Harris are indispensable on this theme: for example 'Social planning in war-time: some aspects of the Beveridge Report', in Jay Winter (ed.), *War and Economic Development*, Cambridge, 1975; *William Beveridge*, Oxford, 1977; and 'Some aspects of social policy in Britain during the Second World War', in W. J. Mommsen (ed.), *The Emergence of the Welfare State in Britain and Germany*, London, 1981.

For the debate about 'war and consensus', see Harold Smith (ed.), *War and Social Change: British Society in the Second World War*, Manchester, 1986; Kevin Jefferys, 'British politics and social policy during the Second World War', *The Historical Journal*, 30, 1, 1987; Rodney Lowe, 'The Second World War, consensus and the foundation of the welfare state', *Twentieth Century British History*, 1, 2, 1990; Dennis Kavanagh and Peter Morris, *Consensus Politics from Attlee to Thatcher*, Oxford, 1989.

Popular politics in wartime

Social histories of the war provide invaluable guidance on popular feeling, most notably Angus Calder's seminal work, *The People's War: Britain 1939–1945*, London, 1969. Calder is particularly strong on Common Wealth; also worth consulting on this theme is D. L. Prynn, 'Common Wealth – a British "third party" of the 1940s', *Journal of Contemporary History*, 7, 1–2, 1972.

On by-election contests, the most important study is Paul Addison, 'By-elections of the Second World War', in Chris Cook and John Ramsden (eds), *By-elections in British Politics*, London, 1973. See also G. H. Bennett, 'The wartime political truce and hopes for post-war coalition: the West Derbyshire by-election, 1944', *Midland History*, 17, 1992.

Two of the more recent attempts to reassess 'the road to 1945' are Richard Sibley, 'The swing to Labour during the Second World War: when and why?', *Labour History Review*, 55, 1, 1990; and Tony Mason and Peter Thompson, ' "Reflections on a Revolution"? The political mood in wartime Britain', in Nick Tiratsoo (ed.), *The Attlee Years*, London, 1991.

The 1945 general election

The most detailed analysis remains R. B. McCullum and Alison Readman, *The British General Election of 1945*, London, 1947, the first of the Nuffield election histories. In spite of its status as a landmark contest, 1945 has not subsequently been researched in any great detail, though important exceptions are: Henry Pelling, 'The 1945 general election reconsidered', *The Historical Journal*, 23, 2, 1980; J. Schneer, 'The Labour left and the general election of 1945', in J. M. W. Bean (ed.), *The Political Culture of Modern Britain*, London, 1987; and Steven Fielding, 'What did "the people" want? The meaning of the 1945 general election', *The Historical Journal*, 35, 3, 1992.

Index